WINVESTING

THE MINIMALIST'S GUIDE TO INDEX FUND INVESTING

JEFF LUKE

DISCLAIMER

The material in this book is for informational purposes only. Nothing in this book constitutes an offer or solicitation of financial advice and is not intended to provide investment, legal, tax, or other professional or financial advice.

Nothing in this book is to be construed as an offer or a recommendation to buy or sell a security. Additionally, the material in this book does not constitute a representation that the investments described herein are suitable or appropriate for any person.

Such content therefore should not be relied upon for the making of any personal financial and investment decisions. Persons accessing this information are strongly encouraged to obtain appropriate professional advice before making any investment or financial decision.

Before investing, please follow these simple guidelines:

1. Never invest in something that you don't understand.
2. Never invest based on anyone else's opinion.
3. Ask for assistance if you need it.

For my dad
My mom
Warren
Steve
Alan
Sam
Ang
Jay
Pia
Lisa
Mira
Mark
Chris
Kevin
Eddie
Shantii
Maximus
Khunploy
And my reader

"I'm always doing things I cannot do, that's how I get to do them." — Picasso

INTRODUCTION

I went from being a bad investor to a good investor when I started investing with index funds. I couldn't believe how simple they were. I'll tell you the main tricks to investing in this book so you don't have to waste years making mistakes.

You might like to know that like you, I have no training as a professional investor. I started investing in my 20s when I became a freelance photographer. I hit the streets of Seattle with a camera in hand, shooting photos for newspapers and magazines. While I was getting my photography business off the ground I knew I needed to put some money aside for the future.

I would write a check for $100 and put it in a stamped envelope to buy mutual fund shares. I did this every month. Invest. Rinse. Repeat. Over the years these hundreds grew into thousands. Nothing too exciting: just writing a check, licking a stamp, sending it off.

You are fortunate because it's much easier to invest today. You can set up an account using your phone or laptop, and then whenever you want to invest you can do it in a few taps or clicks.

I got inspired to write this book because the other day I was talking to a friend, a young photographer who just got out of college and is starting a freelance photography business. He said it's weird that I like both photography and investing because artists usually aren't financial types.

I know what he's talking about, but I think both investing and photography reward those who visualize. The investor is notices, but does not react was the stock market zig-zags up and down, but visualizes their investment's gradual ascent over time. In the same way, a photographer tunes out distractions and visualizes the interplay of light and geometry as they capture a decisive moment.

Both investors and photographers visualize success and keep the important things in focus despite what's happening around them. I think it's no coincidence that photographers and investors both organize their best work in portfolios.

My photographer friend asked, "What's one piece of advice you'd give someone just starting out with investing?"

I thought about it for a second, and then I told him the trick I'm will share with you in these pages.

PART ONE
INDEX FUND INVESTING

ONE

WHAT IS INVESTING?

SIMPLY PUT, investing is putting money to work in a thoughtful way so that it grows into more money in the future.

This book will teach you a minimalist approach to investing. I want to keep things simple because I think that works best for most investors, especially those just starting out.

Now, one method of investing is through an index fund. "What is that?" you might be asking yourself. Well, an index fund is essentially a basket of stocks that an investor can purchase in one simple investment.

But why invest with index funds? An investor in index funds owns a small slice of all the companies in the fund, and many of these companies earn profits, which are reinvested in the business or paid to index fund shareholders as dividends.

I'll tell you why indexing is essential. The last few months I've wanted to buy stock in a few companies I understand well. These are companies I buy stuff from all the time as a photographer, and you might be a customer too. I'm talking about companies like Adobe, Amazon, Apple, Berkshire Hathaway, and Starbucks.

I've had those companies on my list of stocks to buy for a few years, and with the exception of Amazon (I started buying the stock a few years ago) I have not been decisive enough to buy stocks lately because the prices always seemed kind of expensive after a 10 year bull market. I just couldn't decide on which stock was selling for a price that made sense.

Then I finally decided to invest in the Vanguard S&P 500 Index Fund and *voila*, I instantly owned shares of all of the companies listed above, plus 495 other stocks. I had owned shares in the S&P 500 index fund many years ago, and sold those shares (it was a bad idea) so I could buy two individual stocks, which wound up being really crappy stocks. I would have been much better off sticking with an index fund.

As you're reading this book, I think it will help you to keep in mind that throughout history, stocks have marched upward consistently. We have lived through wars, recessions, terror attacks, a financial crisis, and a global pandemic. The stock market always takes a hit, but it recovers. It always seems like the hard times will never end, but they always do.

Successful investors see the wild movements and down around this steady line that they know goes up over the long term. You will be so much better off if you don't try to time the market and jump in and out at the perfect time. No one has successfully timed the market.

Automate your index fund purchases

The great thing about index funds is they let you automate your investing by letting you buy a fixed dollar amount – say $100 or $200 – of index fund shares every month. You can link your bank account to your index fund brokerage account and enter the dollar amount you want to invest every month. Once you've set this up (it takes 2-3 minutes) you can have a set amount of money invested from your bank account into index fund shares on a day of the month that you choose.

This feature is unique to index funds because their share prices are determined after markets close the fund company is able to sell you shares at a set price (it's called the net asset value, or NAV) after the market closes.

It would be impossible to do this with stocks or ETFs because their prices fluctuate during the day, and the fund company or broker wouldn't know what price to give you for an automated trade. Index funds are excellent candidates for investing at regular intervals because they are priced once a day.

The key to investing is consistency and not trying to time the market. Jack Bogle, who founded Vanguard and started the first index fund, said that smart investors tell themselves, "I know I'm not smart enough to get out at the high. I know I'm not smart enough to get back in at the low, so I'm just gonna stay the course, as we would say at Vanguard, and hang on through all that, and importantly, if I'm trying to accumulate money for retirement, or to buy a home, or to educate my children, what you want to do is keep investing."

How to think about investing

It's not your fault that you let the stock market affect how you feel, or make you think now is a time you should invest, or now you should fear investing. The financial media and financial TV shows are always asking you, "Is now is a good time to put money in the market?" They are trying to make you think you should try to time the market. I think this is a big mistake.

It is impossible to time the market. I can't name a single investor who has displayed this ability. Instead, there's a better way to think about investing. You can buy great businesses at good prices. Once you've decided you want to do this, it would be foolish for you not to act because of something you thought the market would do.

Look, it's really hard to pick winning stocks, and it's impossible to time the market. Fortunately for you, you don't have to do either.

Instead, you can decide that you will be a net buyer of stocks over the long term.

This book goes to press at a time of great opportunity. After a 12 year bull market, stocks have become much cheaper. As this book goes to press, the past two months — February and March of 2020 — have provided investors with much lower prices than have existed in years. Picking the perfect moment to buy and knowing which stocks to buy is very hard, but making the easy choice to buy a little part of all of these great stocks is easy.

I think people reading this book, and all investors, will look back on this time as they look back on all steep market sell-offs — as an opportunity to buy stocks at lower prices.

The best way for investors to take advantage of times like these is simply to be a buyer of stocks over a long period of time, especially when stocks of quality companies get cheap.

This book will show you everything you need to know about index funds and how to invest in them. This book is your guide to learning about index funds, and it will teach you the steps to setting up your own account.

Beyond this, you will understand what you're doing, and this will give you the confidence to start investing in index funds if you decide that makes sense for you.

TWO

BASIC FACTS ABOUT INDEX FUNDS

1. Index funds are *passively* managed, which means that their stock holdings mirror the underlying index. These holdings change infrequently, leading to relatively low taxes. In addition, index fund expenses are rock bottom.
2. The S&P 500 index lets you invest in a diverse array of stocks.[1] *Index funds* are often called *passively managed funds,* because they don't actively trade stocks in an attempt to beat the market. Investors can also invest in indexes using exchange-traded index funds (ETFs), which are similar to index funds.
3. Contrary to index funds, *actively managed funds* try to beat the stock market's return by actively trading stocks to optimize performance. These funds often charge high fees and generate higher capital gains taxes than index funds due to their frequent trading. Most actively managed funds trail their indexes.
4. Index funds often have a minimum initial investment of $3,000 to open an account. Many index funds are

available with lower up-front costs as ETFs (starting at the price of one share).
5. Rather than trying to pick which stocks will beat the market, an index fund owns them all.

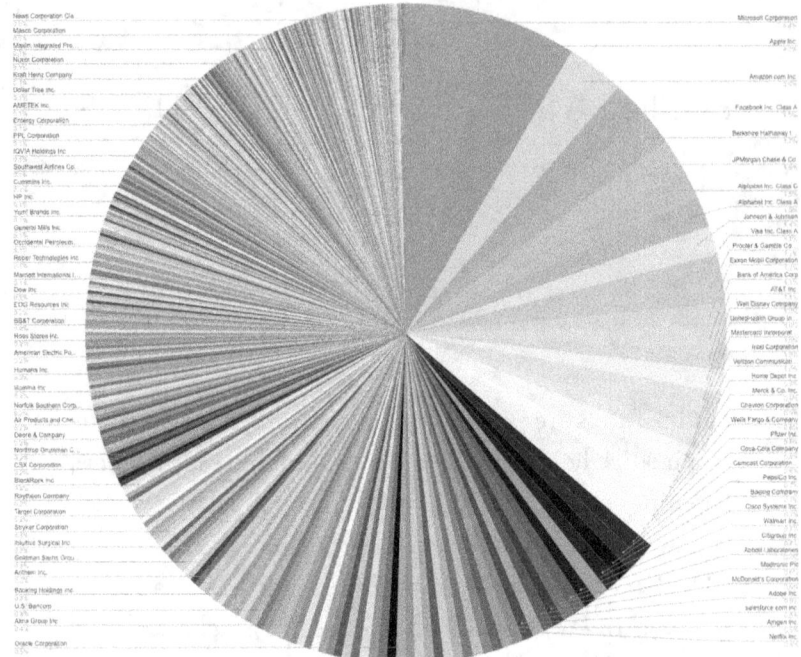

Each slice in this pie chart represents a different company in the S&P 500 Index Fund. You don't need to read each company name, but it's worth noting the wide variety of companies in the index.

LET'S COMPARE THIS S&P 500 index fund with an actively managed fund. Here are the 10 largest stock holdings of Vanguard's S&P 500 index fund, as of this writing,[2] listed in order of the largest stock position (as a percentage of the fund) to the smallest.[3]

Top ten holdings
As of 12/31/2019

1	Apple Inc.	4.6%
2	Microsoft Corp.	4.5%
3	Alphabet Inc.	3.0%
4	Amazon.com Inc.	2.9%
5	Facebook Inc.	1.8%
6	Berkshire Hathaway Inc.	1.7%
7	JPMorgan Chase & Co.	1.6%
8	Johnson & Johnson	1.4%
9	Visa Inc.	1.2%
10	Procter & Gamble Co.	1.2%

Ten largest holdings = 23.90% of total net assets

Vanguard S&P 500 Index Fund holdings. Source: Vanguard website.

As of 12/31/2019, Vanguard S&P 500 Index Fund had 509 stock holdings.[4]

Now let's look at an actively managed fund. Sequoia Fund tries to beat the index while an index fund just passively owns the index. Actively managed funds, as you will see, charge much higher fees and often underperform the indexes.

Sequoia is an example of an *actively managed fund*. Here are the 10 largest holdings of Sequoia fund, which is one of the oldest mutual funds in existence. It had 26 stock holdings at the time of this writing.[5]

TOP 10 HOLDINGS
As of December 31, 2019

Alphabet, Inc.	**12.0%**
Berkshire Hathaway, Inc.	**8.3%**
CarMax, Inc.	**6.2%**
MasterCard, Inc.	**5.3%**
Constellation Software, Inc.	**4.9%**
Jacobs Engineering Group, Inc.	**4.6%**
Credit Acceptance Corp.	**4.6%**
Liberty Broadband Corp.	**4.4%**
Facebook, Inc.	**4.3%**
Liberty Media Corp.	**4.3%**

Sequoia Fund holdings. Source: Sequoia Fund website.

There are some important differences between the two funds listed above:

1. The Vanguard S&P 500 index fund has an annual

expense ratio[6] of .04%, which means that for every $100 you pay $.04 in expenses.
2. The Sequoia Fund has an annual expense ratio of 1.00%.

Now let's look at that difference: *Sequoia Fund costs investors 25x more than Vanguard* because of the expenses they charge to manage your money. That is an enormous difference between index funds and actively managed funds. *Index funds cost less,* meaning you keep more of your money and *pay less in fees.*

Do these expenses matter? Let's take a look at an example comparing $10,000 invested in each of the funds listed above.

The Vanguard 500 index fund charges .04% annually, so that costs $4.00 per year if an investor put in $10,000. This is so cheap it's almost free.

Sequoia Fund charges 1.00% annually, so $10,000 invested costs $100 per year. This is nowhere near as cheap as Vanguard. It's a pretty expensive ongoing cost going to the fund company and not you.

And these fees will only increase as your investment grows, because the fund company always skims a percentage of your total investment.

Mark Twain said, "The difference between the almost right word and the right word is really a large matter — 'Tis the difference between the lightning bug and the lightning." The same could be said of mutual fund fees — *it's a really large matter*.

If one day your investment grows to $100,000 then you would pay Sequoia Fund $1,000 a year! On the other hand, you would only pay the S&P Index Fund $40. It's pretty easy to do the math here. These are recurring fees that are deducted from your account automatically, so most people don't notice them.

The difference between these two funds' expenses is breathtaking: *you would pay Sequoia Fund $960 more than Vanguard each year to manage your money.* Expenses increase as your account grows! These expenses and fees pay fund managers' salaries, but you should aim to keep them for yourself. When it comes to mutual fund fees, *you get what you don't pay for.*

Vanguard S&P 500 Index is the top line, and and Sequoia Fund is the bottom. The index fund is very low cost and its performance was much better than the actively managed Sequoia Fund in the 10 year period reflected in the graph. An investor would have saved a ton in fees and had better performance in the index fund.
Source: Portfolio Visualizer

Now, if Sequoia Fund generated better returns than the Vanguard S&P 500 index then it might make sense to pay more for performance, but higher expenses don't guarantee better performance. In fact, it's usually the other way around: higher expenses result in lower your returns. Also, the Vanguard Fund is diversified across 509 stocks while Sequoia Fund is concentrated in only 26.[7]

The eye-popping difference between actively managed and index funds is that active fund managers have trailed the S&P 500 index for nine years in a row now. When examining the performance over the past decade, 85% of the large-cap funds have underperformed, and after 15 years, nearly 92% have trailed the index.[8]

THREE

WHERE CAN YOU BUY INDEX FUNDS & ETFS?

INDEX FUNDS and ETFs are available through brokerage firms or directly through fund companies, and these, especially ETFs, have become enormously popular in recent years.

I look for low costs when researching the companies that offer index funds and ETFs, since I believe that annual expenses should be as low as possible.

I mainly discuss Vanguard funds in this book because I'm more familiar with them, given that I am a long-term shareholder of their funds. The company is owned by its shareholders, which means that the company does not have a corporate parent that it has to satisfy with profits. Vanguard has a long history and storied reputation for providing quality service to its customers.

While I like Vanguard's low cost structure and customer service, there are many other reputable companies like Fidelity, Schwab, and many others that offer index funds and ETFs that may interest you. Just because Vanguard makes sense for me doesn't mean it's the best fit for you. I encourage you to consider your options before investing.

Similarities between ETFs & Mutual Funds

You may be surprised by the similarities shared by ETFs and mutual funds, the biggest similarity being that ETFs and mutual funds both represent professionally managed collections, or "baskets", of individual stocks and bonds.

They are both less risky than investing in individual stocks or bonds, and they are both overseen by professional money managers.[1]

What is an ETF?

An ETF is an investment that's built like a mutual fund—investing in potentially hundreds, sometimes even thousands, of individual securities—but it trades on an exchange throughout the day, much like a stock.[2]

What's the difference between an ETF and a mutual fund?

There are more similarities than differences between ETFs and mutual funds. But the biggest differences are that:

ETFs have lower investment minimums. An ETF's minimum is the price of a single share, which could be as little as $50 depending on the ETF, while a mutual fund may require $1,000, $3,000, or more to get started.

ETFs have more transparent pricing in real-time, so you can see their prices change throughout the trading day. A mutual fund isn't priced until the trading day is over, so you don't know your price until after you've placed your trade.[3]

You will experience low-cost investing whether you invest with an index fund or an ETF. Just the simple fact that you are investing will have a much greater impact on your financial future than the choice between an index fund and its corresponding ETF.

For the sake of keeping things simple, I will provide you with all of the information that I would want to have when making an investment decision. If you would like further details on the differences between index funds and ETFs you can find them on Vanguard's website.[4]

Index Funds vs. ETFs - Which is Better?

Index funds and ETFs are like twins—just not identical twins. They're alike because they both offer an inexpensive way to buy a diversified basket of stocks or bonds, and they have lower costs than actively managed mutual funds.

Deciding which one is better varies from person to person, but I'm going to outline the main points right here to hopefully give you a decent idea about which one is the right fit for you.

A Few Factors to Consider

- ETFs have lower minimum investments than index mutual funds, making them easier for beginners.
- ETFs usually have expense ratios less than or equal to comparable index mutual funds, although these differences are usually insignificant.
- Index funds trade once per day, after the market closes, so investors have less control over price. ETFs trade like stocks, so investors can buy and sell them during the day like they would with stocks.
- Index funds allow shareholders to automatically reinvest their dividends. ETFs don't usually offer that service. The Vanguard Brokerage dividend reinvestment program is a free service that lets you reinvest capital gains and dividend distributions in additional shares of the same ETF.[5]

Why you might like an index fund: If you want to automate

investing at regular intervals, index mutual funds make sense. You can link your bank account to your investment account to have a set amount invested monthly.

One obstacle to index fund investing, however, may be the high minimum initial investment required to open an account. Many mutual funds require $2,500 or $3,000, which can be a lot of money for those who are just starting out. You can invest in an ETF for the price of a single share, which is much less than the minimums to open an index fund.

Why you might like an ETF: If you want to control the exact time during the trading day that you buy shares, then you'll prefer an ETF because it trades throughout the day just like a stock.

FOUR

HOW TO INVEST IN INDEX FUNDS

I WANT to show you how to get started investing in an index fund. To make investing easy, I will show you what you'll see if you visit Vanguard's website.[1]

Here are the steps needed in order to set up an account to start investing in an index fund:

Vanguard 500 Index Fund Admiral Shares
(VFIAX)

Month-end holdings
as of 12/31/2019

Rank/holdings	Percentage
1 Apple Inc.	4.60%
2 Microsoft Corp.	4.50%
3 Alphabet Inc.	3.00%
4 Amazon.com Inc.	2.90%
5 Facebook Inc.	1.80%
6 Berkshire Hathaway Inc.	1.70%
7 JPMorgan Chase & Co.	1.60%
8 Johnson & Johnson	1.40%
9 Visa Inc.	1.20%
10 Procter & Gamble Co.	1.20%

10 largest holdings = 23.90% of total net assets

Portfolio holdings may exclude any temporary cash investments and stock index products.

Vanguard portfolio holdings disclaimer

Open your account online

This shows you the name of an index fund, its 10 largest holdings, and a red bar with "Open your account online".

Vanguard

What would you like to do?

Welcome to a different way of thinking—and feeling—about investing.

Open a new account

Select an account type that works for your goals, such as saving for retirement (an IRA), general investing, or saving for education (a 529 account).

Let's open my account

When you click the bar to open your account online you're given a few options.

Vanguard

How will you fund this new account?

○ Electronic bank transfer or another Vanguard account.

○ Rollover from an employer plan.

○ Transfer investments from another financial firm.

[Continue]

A few ways to fund your index fund investing account.

Open an account

Things you'll need

✓ The routing and your account number at your bank (if not already on file).

✓ Your current employer's name and address (required by law).

This screen lets you know a few things you'll need to set up your account.

New account process

Choose an account type

Retirement (IRA, annuity); general savings (individual, joint, trust); education (529, UGMA/UTMA); small business (i401(k), SIMPLE, SEP).

Complete our online application (5–10 minutes)

We'll open your account and initiate a transfer from your bank (if applicable).

Watch for a confirmation (1–2 days)

We'll email you status updates throughout the process as well as a confirmation when we receive your funds. Once your account is funded, you can choose Vanguard investments as well as individual stocks, bonds, and ETFs.

The steps in the new account process.

Setting up an account is a simple process. The website is self-explanatory, and if you prefer you can download the Vanguard App and use your phone.

Keep in mind that if you want to invest in an ETF (this is useful if you don't have enough money to meet the minimum initial investment amount) then you'll need a brokerage account.

The next chapter shows you the steps to buy ETFs once you've established a Vanguard Brokerage Services (VBS) account.

FIVE

HOW TO INVEST IN ETFS

26 JEFF LUKE

🔍 Positions

VOO
Vanguard SP 500 ETF

Last trade PSE	$302.03 -2.78 (-0.91%) 01/24/2020 04:00 PM ET
Bid / Ask — —	$0.0 / $0.0
Size / Tick	0x0 / —
Volume	3,448,207
Account type	Cash
Shares	1
	Dollars to shares calculator >
Order type	Limit >
Limit price	$303.00
Duration	Day >

Quotes are shown in real time during regular trading hours. Market data provided by Thomson Reuters. Data are provided for information purposes only and are not intended for trading purposes. Thomson Reuters shall not be liable for any errors or any delay in the content, or for any action taken in reliance thereon. The RIC Thomson Reuters Instrument Code set has been developed and maintained by Thomson Reuters and is the intellectual property of Thomson Reuters. For additional quote information, go to the security profile page.

CANCEL   **CONTINUE**

These are actual screenshots taken from my phone. As you can see, I've entered the ticker symbol VOO. The last price per share was $302.03. I have placed an order to buy 1 share as a limit order, with a limit price of $303.00. This ensures that an investor will pay any amount up to the limit price (in this case, $303.00) and it protects an investor from paying more than expected for their share(s). As long as the price for a share is below $303.00 and I have enough funds in my brokerage account to fund the purchase, this trade will execute. I have selected "Day" as the duration, which means the trade has to occur during the day the order is placed, otherwise it is cancelled. If everything is correct, you can click "continue."

Review and submit	
ORDER SUMMARY	
Transaction type	Buy
Symbol	VOO Vanguard S&P 500 ETF
Shares	1
Order type	Limit
Limit price	$303.00
Duration	Day
Account type	Cash
ESTIMATED TRANSACTION DETAILS	
Estimated principal	$303.00
Estimated commission	$0.00
Estimated net amount	$303.00

After you enter the details of your "buy" order you are then brought to this "Review and submit" page to confirm the transaction type, symbol (which is VOO for the Vanguard S&P 500 ETF), number of shares, limit price (if you set one), and duration.

← Review and submit

ORDER SUMMARY

Shares	1
Order type	Limit
Limit price	$303.00
Duration	Day
Account type	Cash

ESTIMATED TRANSACTION DETAILS

Estimated principal	$303.00
Estimated commission	$0.00
Estimated net amount	$303.00

The commission and principal amounts are estimates. Market fluctuation, commission changes, availability of last price, or other changes may impact the final commission or principal amount. You'll receive final confirmation with transaction details for all executed trades.

Industry regulations require securities to be delivered on the settlement date. Vanguard reserves the right to reject your order at any time, for any reason, and without prior notice. If you continue this transaction, please monitor your order status to determine the final disposition of your order. You're liable for covering all transactions placed in this account. If you choose to exchange Vanguard funds into your money market settlement fund to cover this trade, you must complete the transaction no later than the business day before the settlement date. For market orders, you should consider price volatility when determining whether you'll have sufficient assets to pay for your purchase.

By clicking Submit, you consent to electronic access to the prospectus of the security you're purchasing. You may view and print the prospectus after submitting your order. If you would like an additional paper copy, please call Vanguard at 800-992-8327.

CANCEL   SUBMIT

Scroll down to verify transaction details and estimated trade costs. Then click "SUBMIT" to enter your order to buy ETF share(s).

AS YOU CAN SEE, the steps are pretty easy to follow. You will also have the opportunity to verify that everything is correct after entering the trade information.

Here are a few portfolios that I think make sense for beginners.

The pie chart below shows a portfolio with 90% allocated to the Vanguard 500 Index Fund (VFIAX) and 10% allocated to the Vanguard Short-Term Treasury Index Fund (VSBSX). Both funds have $3,000 minimums. If you don't want to pay these minimums then you can purchase the corresponding ETFs.

SIX

TWO ESSENTIAL INVESTMENTS

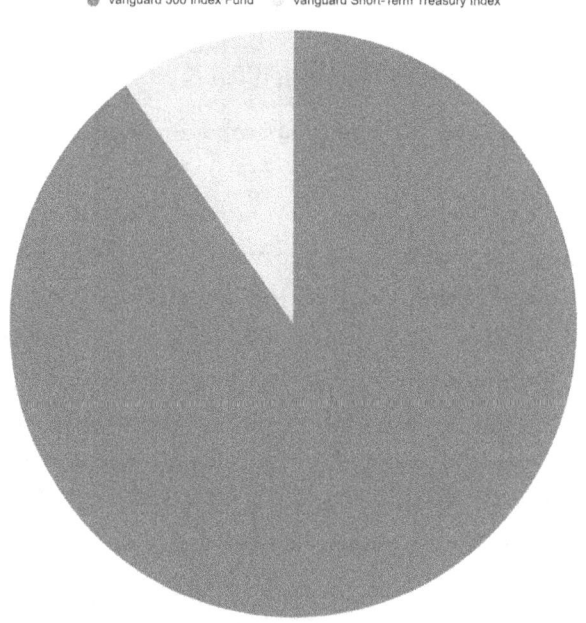

90% Vanguard 500 Index Fund (VFIAX) and 10%
Vanguard Short-Term Treasury Index (VSBSX).

FOR THE VANGUARD S&P 500 Index Fund:
   The ticker symbol is **VFIAX**
   If you prefer the ETF, the corresponding ticker is **VOO**
   For the Short-Term Treasury Index Fund:
   The ticker symbol is **VSBSX**
   If you prefer the ETF, the corresponding ticker is **VGSH**

Alternatives to the Short-Term Treasury Fund

If you prefer to use a *money market fund* or a *savings account* for the non-stock part of your investments those are also suitable investments instead of a short-term treasury fund. The main concept here is you want a risk-free investment so you can get your hands on the money if you need it. Any insured bank account or money market account should provide the liquidity and ease of access you need.

Buffett's Instructions to Wife's Trustees

In the 2014 Berkshire Hathaway shareholder letter, Warren Buffett shared his instructions to the trustees of the money he will be leaving to his wife.

I'm sharing this information because it's the advice Buffett shares with those who ask him how to invest their money. He said one bequest in his will provides that cash will be delivered to a trustee for his wife's benefit, and his advice to the trustee could not be more simple: Put 10% of the cash in short-term government bonds and 90% in a very low-cost S&P 500 index fund (Buffett suggests Vanguard's). Buffett said he believes the trust's long-term results from this policy will be superior to those attained by most investors.

You can get started with investing if that's what you want to do. It's not hard, and I know you have what it takes to get started. Even if you've never invested before, I know you have what it takes to set up an index fund account or buy your first ETF shares to become an investor.

If you take anything with you at all from this first section, I hope you'll remember the following:

- Amateur investors will get a perfectly decent return if they simply invest in an unmanaged, low-cost index fund.
- If you want to automate investing at regular intervals you can invest in an index fund, such as the Vanguard S&P 500 Index fund (VFIAX).
- If you want to buy the same fund but prefer the ETF version you can invest in the Vanguard S&P 500 Index ETF, with the ticker symbol VOO.
- Index investors don't have to spend lots of time researching companies.
- You get instant diversification across the 500 largest companies in the United States all in just a single fund.

SEVEN
A SURPRISING REVEAL

FOR YEARS I thought that these investors' returns could easily beat the S&P 500 index, and I falsely believed that an S&P 500 index fund was the easy choice for know-nothing investors. But I've come to realize that it's the smart choice for everyone — even highly skilled investors.

1. Early in my investing career I believed the hype that highly paid mutual fund managers were worth their high fees; this belief was incorrect.
2. The financial media accepts advertising money from mutual fund companies to mutual fund managers in contests based on short-term performance. These are little more than advertising gimmicks and popularity contests.

Most mutual fund companies are simply marketing machines where funds are basically an afterthought. These companies pump their funds in glossy business magazines and their five-star ratings are plastered all over newspaper ads, magazines, and financial websites.

What Happens to Mutual Funds with Poor Records?

What happens to the unsuccessful mutual funds? Oftentimes, they are closed and their losing records vanish. These black sheep are banished from the herd and their dismal performance disappears. The surviving funds then give off the impression that all of a fund company's children are above average.

EIGHT
TED & TODD'S RETURNS ALMOST BEAT THE S&P 500 INDEX

MY BIGGEST SURPRISE when writing this book came while I was watching a video where Warren Buffett revealed the stock returns of his handpicked protégés at Berkshire Hathaway.

It made me realize that even the smartest investors on the planet can't easily beat the S&P.

The discovery I made while watching that video interview with Warren Buffett[1] occurred when Becky Quick asked him to answer a viewer's question about Todd Combs and Ted Weschler, two genius investors who Buffett handpicked as his protégés to pick stocks for Berkshire Hathaway.

The question was this: *"How are Ted and Todd's performance since they joined about eight years ago? Have they performed better than the index? Charlie (Munger) said recently that most managers did not add any value compared to an index."*

Buffett's answer: "The first few years each of 'em - they came at a slightly different time - maybe a year or a year and a half or something, different times. They got well ahead of the index and they got paid compensation so it came in thirds, so that it could be clawed back 2/3 of it if they missed the second year, and so on. Overall they are a tiny bit behind the S&P, each, by just almost the same margin, over the same time — over the entire period, and the entire period is a little different for both of them. They now manage about $13 billion each. They've done better than I have."

Did you catch that? For the past eight years, Ted and Todd, who Warren Buffett hand-picked to invest "...*are a tiny bit behind the S&P over the same time.*" And both of them have done better than Buffett.

The fact that many of the best investors on the planet can't beat the S&P 500 index should make you celebrate like squirrels at a piñata party. The returns you get with a low-cost S&P 500 index fund will likely crush the returns of the world's top investors.
Illustration by Edwin Yaguar Chávez

Think about that for a second. *The best professional investors Buffett could find did not beat the S&P during their first eight years on the job.*

If we flip the script, what we're really saying is that the S&P outperformed Warren Buffett and his two expert stock-pickers.

NINE
YOU GET WHAT YOU DON'T PAY FOR

WITH MOST THINGS IN LIFE, the saying rings true: you get what you pay for.

With mutual funds and ETFs, however, you get what you *don't* pay for![1]

Both index and actively managed funds fish from the same pond.

With any investment fund you get to keep the market's return *minus the fees and expenses* charged by the fund management company. The less the fund company takes, the more you keep. So you will, of course, want to reduce fees wherever possible.

The image below was inspired by a talk I heard Warren Buffett give about index funds. I made this image to illustrate the point he made when he said that all investors, whether index fund investors or stock pickers, invest from the same *universe* of stocks.

A stock picker or active manager can't outperform index funds consistently because all investors own the same universe of stocks. An investor's returns can't exceed those of the overall universe. Therefore, it makes sense to own stocks on a low-cost basis.

An investor's returns can never exceed those of the overall universe. Therefore, it makes sense to own stocks on a low-cost basis.

Active fund managers can't consistently outperform the market because *they are the market.* They fish from the same pond as index funds and ETFs, but their returns suffer because they are reduced by the *sales commissions, annual expenses, and taxes* consumed by their costly funds.

If you take anything with you at all from this section, I hope you'll remember the following:

- Ted & Todd, Buffett's handpicked protégés at Berkshire

Hathaway, have proven that it is incredibly difficult to beat the index.
- Superstar mutual fund managers seldom provide consistently good performance. Most have hot streaks followed by poor performance.
- Investment managers pick from the same universe of stocks that you can own when you buy shares of the S&P 500 index fund or ETF.

TEN

THE MIGHTY SEQUOIA

I REMEMBER LEARNING about Sequoia Fund when I was in my early 20s and just getting my feet wet with investing. It had a great record and was in high demand, but unfortunately it was closed to new investors. Imagine having your money and wanting an investment firm to invest it for you, but they wouldn't take your money! An extremely rare trait on Wall Street.

There are few reasons a manager closes a fund, and it's usually a sign of a well-run fund company closing a fund before it gets too big, since size often hinders performance.

In this story I'm going to share with you how one small mistake can ruin a great record. What was once among the most successful and exclusive mutual funds in the world quickly fell from grace when its managers loaded up on one bad stock.

Before we dive deep into the coming disaster at Sequoia Fund, I just want to make a distinction that I think will be helpful to those readers new to mutual funds.

As you may recall, index funds are a type of mutual fund that are passively managed to mirror a benchmark like the S&P 500. The trading within an index fund portfolio is low, but on the other hand, actively managed mutual funds are run by managers who try and pick stocks that will beat a benchmark like the S&P 500.

There are a handful of fund managers lauded by the financial media as the "managers of their decade."[1] These managers and their funds' performance often garner press coverage, which thereby increases the cash flowing into these funds in order to chase past performance; in most cases the previous performance does not persist.

Earlier, we compared the *expenses* of the Vanguard S&P 500 Index ownership to Sequoia Fund, but we did not discuss the topic of performance — how much money the fund returns to you, the investor.

ELEVEN

I WANTED TO INVEST IN SEQUOIA

WHEN I FIRST LOOKED AT Sequoia Fund's excellent track record in Forbes Magazine's Annual Mutual Fund Survey, I wished I could invest in that fund. It was one of the top-performing mutual funds with a stunning long-term record. Unfortunately, the fund was closed to new investors and I wasn't on the guest list.

Although I couldn't invest in the fund, I admired Sequoia Fund's outstanding performance from afar. From the beginning of 2000 through July 2015, Sequoia earned 10.1% annualized returns, crushing the S&P 500 index by an average of 5.8% per year.[1]

I grew curious as to why Sequoia Fund was doing so well during this stretch when no other funds were beating the averages like Sequoia. A quick Google search revealed that the fund's largest stake was Valeant Pharmaceuticals, which represented 32% of Sequoia's assets. That begged the question: What did Sequoia know about Valeant to have such confidence?

Valeant's soaring share price helped Sequoia trounce the market from 2010 through to 2013, a feat that only one-third of actively managed US funds could claim during that time.[2]

I thought maybe Sequoia's research analysts had special connections in the world of finance to deeply understand the magic that was Valeant. I couldn't have been more wrong.

TWELVE
SEQUOIA FUND DISASTER

SEQUOIA'S INVESTMENT managers got fooled... big time. They *thought* they understood Valeant better than they did when the allegations surfaced in 2015 that Valeant's success may have been built on price gouging, a secret network of specialty pharmacies, and fraud. As a result, Valeant's stock plunged more than 60% in three months.[1]

Sequoia Fund suffered gargantuan losses because of their misplaced bet on Valeant Pharmaceuticals. The stock plunged 93% from August 2015 to June 2016 as the controversial drug manufacturer faced scrutiny over its business practices.[2]

Over time, Sequoia Fund fell 34%, lagging behind Standard & Poor's 500-stock index by 31 percentage points.[3] Valeant, one of Wall Street's hottest stocks for years, was a disastrous investment for Sequoia, hedge funds, and Wall Street's so-called smart money that was piled into the stock as the company's revenue skyrocketed.[4]

The graph below shows the performance of Sequoia Fund (bottom) versus the S&P 500 (top). Sequoia's assets, $9.3 billion at their peak, now stand at $3.9 billion.[5] Going "all in" to Valeant with 32% of the fund's assets is shows the problem that arose because Sequoia invested in a company it did not understand. This graph is a visual representation of a fatal investing car crash.

If you look at the growth of $10,000 on the right side of the chart you'll see that just owning the index fund strategy would leave you with $21,133 more than if you had invested with the once-great Sequoia Fund during that period.

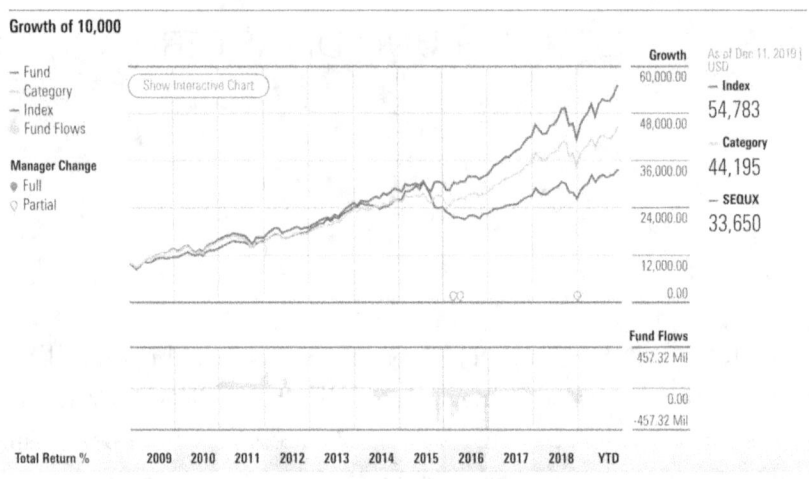

Sequoia's wager was a risky, real-life example of the world of investing on what happens when you bet too heavily on a stock you do not understand. Chart from morningstar.com

THIRTEEN
THE LESSON YOU CAN LEARN

IF YOU'RE CONSIDERING INVESTING in the S&P 500, the positive lesson to be learned is not the severity of Sequoia's mistake, but how splendidly the S&P performed in comparison. Look at the image below and find the "+/- Index" and you'll see that Sequoia Fund underperformed the S&P 500 index in 2009, 2014, 2015, 2016, 2017, and 2018.[1] In other words, the S&P 500 index fund *beat* Sequoia in all of those years, cost 1/25th as much, and owned a diversified set of 510 different stocks, as opposed to only 21 with Sequoia.

Total Return %	2009	2010	2011	2012	2013	2014	2015	2016	2017	2018	YTD
Fund	15.38	19.50	13.19	15.68	34.58	7.55	-7.29	-6.90	20.06	-2.62	27.48
+/- Category	-20.30	3.97	15.65	0.34	0.66	-2.45	-10.90	-10.13	-7.61	-0.53	-0.82
+/- Index	-21.83	2.78	10.55	0.42	1.09	-5.50	-12.96	-13.98	-10.16	-1.11	-4.71
Quartile Rank											
Percentile Rank	97	7	1	42	42	78	98	97	92	54	62
# of Funds in Cat.	1,796	1,718	1,683	1,681	1,712	1,710	1,681	1,463	1,363	1,405	1,366

YTD Fund as of Dec 06, 2019 | Category: Large Growth as of Dec 06, 2019 | Index: Russell 1000 Growth TR USD as of Dec 06, 2019

The Vanguard S&P 500 Index Fund *beat* Sequoia in all of those years, cost 1/25th as much, and owned 510 different stocks compared to only 21 with Sequoia. *Image from morningstar.com*

Trailing Returns

	1-Day	1-Week	1-Month	3-Month	YTD	1-Year	3-Year	5-Year	10-Year	15-Year
Total Return %	0.78	-0.01	2.67	3.60	27.48	23.49	14.22	5.14	11.34	7.93
+/- Category	-0.03	0.20	-0.78	-0.71	-0.82	3.83	-2.95	-6.17	-1.99	-1.31
+/- Index	-0.09	0.15	-0.81	-2.01	-4.71	0.30	-5.44	-8.58	-3.72	-2.47

You can see by looking at the +/- Index" row at the bottom that Sequoia's 3-Year, 5-Year, 10-Year, and 15-Year returns all lag behind the S&P 500 Index Fund. Image from morningstar.com

Sequoia is an example of a shining star of the fund world that shined too brightly before crashing and burning. The fund's 46-year-old record was destroyed in the blink of an eye. That one horrible decision ruined the firm's reputation and caused staggering shareholder losses.

Any investor that depends on a fund manager to exhibit intelligence runs the risk of them doing something stupid. Even if it's just one bad choice, it can harm the fund. On the other hand, Index fund investors are protected from any single stock sinking the ship. With 500 funds in the S&P, any one failure has a negligible effect on overall returns.

In case you think that Sequoia's malaise was an isolated event, I want to show you five other mutual funds that exhibited market-beating returns for many years and brought their managers' fame in the pages of Forbes, the Wall Street Journal, and in the Morningstar surveys of best managers.

The funds below have had (or had—Wintergreen Fund has since closed) mutual fund managers who attracted media coverage, awards and emoluments, and built great records (with the sole exception of Wintergreen fund) before their investing trains derailed, leaving investors with market-lagging results.

I'd been tempted at one time to invest in one of the funds below, but fortunately I never pulled the trigger. I share these examples of once-famous funds that fell from grace, so you can see the disasters you can avoid if you avoid actively managed funds and stick with S&P 500 index funds.

These funds are marketing machines. They have all received a lot of financial headlines in Forbes, Morningstar, and other financial media outlets. These funds also share something else in common: each one sucks like an airplane toilet.

All of the funds listed below charge expenses that are many times higher than those charged by an S&P 500 index fund.

FOURTEEN

ONCE GREAT ACTIVELY MANAGED FUNDS THAT FLOPPED

1. *Wintergreen Fund*

David Winters' Wintergreen Fund was a fairly popular fund in the early 2000s, and the manager touted his "deep value" style on TV shows like Consuelo Mack's WealthTrack. Winters' fund charged high expenses and he threw shade on index funds during an appearance on WealthTrack when he said, "Index funds are more expensive, higher risk and less diversified than you have been led to believe."[1]

Wintergreen Fund was many times more expensive than index funds, and its returns were far worse. I recently searched for some information about the fund and discovered that Wintergreen Fund closed up shop in 2019. The fund's board of directors approved the liquidation on April 15, and it took effect after the market closed on April 17. According to the fund's website, it "has suspended most sales of its shares pending the completion of the liquidation and the payment of liquidating distributions to its shareholders."[2]

While the S&P 500 index fund (top line) climbed steadily, Wintergreen Fund (bottom line) performed poorly during the past decade. The fund landed at the bottom of its Morningstar category over the 1-, 3-, 5-, and 10-year periods. Chart: Yahoo Finance.

An article in Barron's Magazine about the closing of Wintergreen Fund mentioned that Winters' investing style did not fare well in the past decade, and his fund landed at the absolute bottom of its Morningstar category over the 1-, 3-, 5-, and 10-year periods.[3]

When I look back on Winter's disparaging comments about index funds I think he spoke out of self-interest: his own mutual fund lagged far behind the S&P 500 index. He was throwing stones at the index fund that delivered better returns at a lower cost.

Winters criticized Warren Buffett with regard to equity compensation to executives at Coca-Cola (Buffett sits on Coke's board of directors). Speaking of Winters, Buffett said, "When David Winters, who runs a fund that has underperformed by every measure from inception, five years, one year, and who draws a 150 basis point fee when you can go to Vanguard and do it for 17 basis points and he complains about compensation not being commensurate with performance at Coke. And then he has that kind of record himself, I think he's a fellow living in an all-glass house."[4]

. . .

2. *Muhlenkamp Fund*

Ron Muhlenkamp founded the mutual fund that achieved remarkable success and won Forbes Magazine's prestigious "Honor Roll" ranking. This fund was featured in Forbes' prestigious list of mutual funds that performed well in rising markets and preserved value in down markets for seven years in a row, from 2000 to 2007.

Once a standout in the mutual fund world, Muhlenkamp Fund has fallen mightily since its glory days. Just take a look at its relatively poor performance:

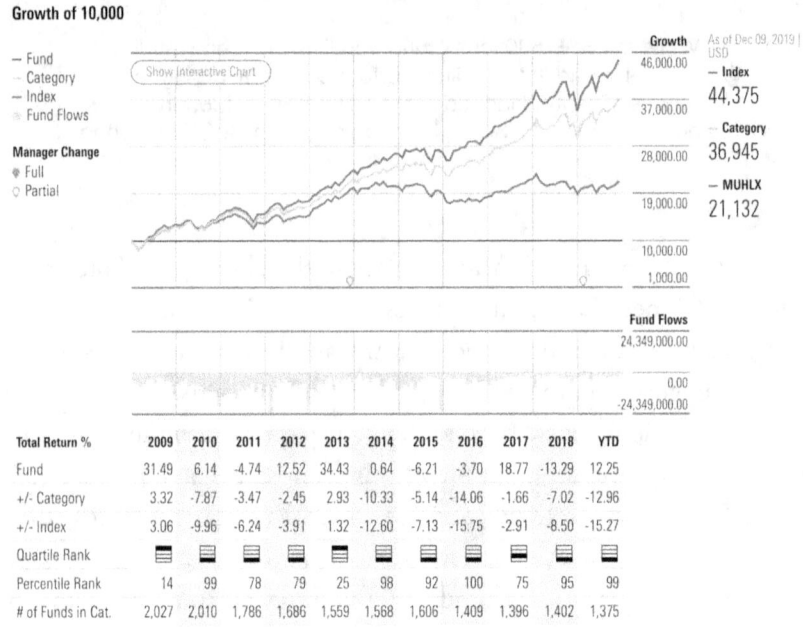

The Vanguard S&P 500 Index (top line) and the Muhlenkamp Fund (bottom line) for 10 years, from 2009 through December 9, 2019. Graph and Chart from morningstar.com.

The top line shows the S&P 500 Index, while the bottom line shows the Muhlenkamp fund. In the rising stock market, $10,000 grew to $44,375 in ten years in the low-cost index fund and $21,132 with Muhlenkamp. The Vanguard S&P 500 Index Fund charges .04% annual expenses, and the Muhlenkamp Fund charges 1.13%.[5]

In other words, Muhlenkamp Fund charges 28 times as much as the index fund for market-lagging performance.

3. *Fairholme Fund* is managed Bruce Berkowitz, who won Morningstar's first-ever "Fund Manager of the Decade" award for the period from 2000-2010. In the decade after he received the award, Berkowitz' Fairholme Fund severely underperformed the S&P 500 index. Large bets on Sears Holdings, St. Joe's, Fannie Mae, and Freddie Mac contributed to staggering losses at Fairholme Fund.

	1-Day	1-Week	1-Month	3-Month	YTD	1-Year	3-Year	5-Year	10-Year
Total Return %	-0.40	-0.80	6.72	2.86	31.46	31.98	-1.85	1.02	4.69
+/- Category	-0.33	-1.00	4.36	-4.99	6.29	5.96	-11.43	-6.72	-6.12
+/- Index	-0.37	-1.02	4.34	-4.91	4.86	4.43	-11.12	-7.01	-6.98

Fairholme Fund has lagged behind the S&P 500 index for the past 3-, 5-, 10-, and 15-year time periods, according to Morningstar. Chart / morningstar.com

Investors poured billions of dollars into the fund in an attempt to chase the manager's early returns, and after the big bets went south they ran for the exits. Berkowitz went from receiving the "Best Fund Manager of the Decade" award to severe underperformance. Fairholme fund has lagged behind the S&P 500 index for the past 3-, 5-, 10-, and 15-year time periods, according to Morningstar[6].

4. *Legg Mason Value Trust*, managed by Bill Miller, whose mutual fund handily beat the S&P 500 for 15 consecutive years at the turn of the century, is riding off into the sunset after his recent lagging returns left a trail of disappointed investors. When he left the fund in 2016, its 1-year return of -18.06% lagged 98% of its peers and trailed the 5.73% advance of the S&P 500 Index during that period, according to Morningstar.[7]

. . .

5. *CGM Focus Fund*, run by star fund manager Ken Heebner, was widely regarded as one of the best mutual fund managers around. CGM Focus Fund's 1-year return of -21.35% lagged 100% of its peers. Put another way, $10,000 invested in 2009 returned $44,442 in the Vanguard S&P 500 Index and grew to a paltry $12,701 in CGM Focus Fund. That's an epic failure.[8]

These examples above underscore the fact that the performance of actively managed funds seldom persists.

If you take anything with you at all from this section, I hope you'll remember the following:

- Great actively managed funds often fail because of dumb mistakes or the fund's investment style falling out of favor for prolonged periods of time.
- Star managers' superior performance seldom persists
- Index fund returns outperform those of most professional investors.

FIFTEEN
TEMPERAMENT IS KEY TO YOUR SUCCESS

YOU'LL DO WELL as an investor if you develop a sense of equanimity. This is the grace under pressure of the ship captain sailing rough seas. You must keep your eye on the horizon and your hand at the wheel.

There will be times when others panic and worry about things beyond their control, but you must not be swayed by the emotions of the crowd.

A calm temperament is the key to your success. So to succeed when markets are crashing down around you and panic is in the air don't worry about things that are out of your hands.

Only Focus on Things Within Your Control

To WIN at investing, just remember:

1. The investments you select, as well as when you buy them, are *entirely under your control*.
2. The economy and stock market *not within your control*, so just remain calm despite the vicissitudes of life. If the

market crashes, you should love the opportunity to take advantage of wild swings.

If you can remember these two truths you will be at a tremendous advantage compared to most people.

This chart shows the S&P 500 index over the past 90 years, with the recessions indicated by shaded areas. Despite the Great Depression, two world wars, terrorist attacks, and several financial crises, the stock market has continued to move *up*!

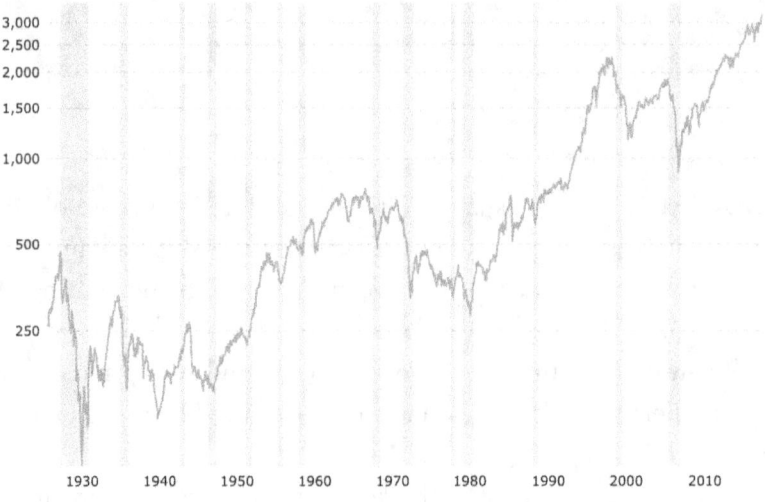

S&P 500 Index - 90 Year Historical Chart. Source: Macrotrends.net

The patient investor who sat still and did nothing despite the crashes and recessions did well over the long-term. With that in mind, remember the perspective of the philosopher Baruch Spinoza, who said: "You must look at things in the aspect of eternity." Maintain a view of the big picture, knowing that companies in the United States will grow their profits over time, and your ownership stake will increase in value.

Charlie Munger explains how he and Warren Buffett run Berkshire Hathaway:

"Our system is to swim as competently as we can and sometimes the tide will be with us and sometimes it will be against us. But by and large we don't much bother with trying to predict the tides because we plan to play the game for a long time."

Munger suggests it's a delusion to outguess macroeconomic cycles, because very few people do it successfully and some of them do it by accident. "When the game is that tough," he said, "why not adopt the other system of swimming as competently as you can and figuring that over a long life you'll have your share of good tides and bad tides?"

SIXTEEN

MY OWN INVESTING STORY

I STARTED INVESTING when I was 25, and I read everything I could about investing. I started with Forbes Magazine, and I read an article about mutual fund investing. I thought that made the most sense to me because I didn't know anything at all about investing in the stock market.

I made an initial investment of $1,000 (the minimum you needed to start an account) and after that I decided to add $100 each month. I was just starting out as a professional photographer at the time, and I certainly wasn't earning boatloads, but I made enough to save and invest every month. I just wanted to have enough money to fix my car if it broke down, to pay rent, and not go into credit card debt.

What you're reading in these pages is the real-life experience from someone who has tried this out and is living proof that it works. I attribute a lot of the success to having the right temperament and not getting spooked by the market crash in 2000 and the financial crisis in 2008. I stayed calm and continued to invest when stocks got cheap.

Sure, I've made some mistakes along the way, but having a good temperament to continue investing in both the good times and bad—

especially in the bad—kept me on track. If you stay calm with your plan to invest in the S&P over many years, you'll do just fine.

> *"Through chances various, through all vicissitudes, we make our way."*
>
> *AENEID*

Those lines from the Aeneid will help you keep the right mindset not only through investing but through all of the terrible, hard blows in life. Here's a poem I learned about from Charlie Munger that talks about being prepared when trouble comes.

SEVENTEEN
PREPARE FOR TROUBLE

CHARLIE MUNGER HAS OFTEN SAID that he has gone through life preparing himself for hard times. He said that it's helped him in many ways. He says this poem by A.E. Houseman captures his own personal approach to being ready for the peregrinations of life and the market.

> "The thoughts of others
> Were light and fleeting,
> Of lovers' meeting
> Or luck or fame.
> Mine were of trouble,
> And mine were steady;
> So I was ready
> When trouble came."
>
> *A.E. HOUSEMAN*

Munger explains his affinity for the poem:

"You can say, who wants to go through life anticipating trouble? Well, I did. All my life I've gone through life anticipating trouble. And here I am, going along in my 84th year and like Epictetus, I've had a favored life. It didn't make me unhappy to anticipate trouble all the time and be ready to perform adequately if trouble came. It didn't hurt me at all. In fact it helped me."

If you take anything with you at all from this section, I hope you'll remember the following:

- Focus only on the things within your control.
- Think of investing beyond this week or month; think in terms of years and decades.
- Prepare yourself for life's stormy weather and just keep a cool head. Have some same cash saved to buy stocks cheaply during the market's wild swings.

PART TWO
GO TO THE NEXT LEVEL

EIGHTEEN

FOCUS WITH FUNDS

NOW WE'RE GOING to go to the next level with index funds.

Instead of just investing in the 500 index, we'll look at ways to improve your investment returns by focusing on specific sectors of the stock market.

You first have to realize that this is not required. Some might even say that you're messing with success if you already know the "base case" of investing in the 500 index, and your expected return will be almost identical to the market's return. So if you start to try and improve your returns, you're betting that you know something about stocks or the future that the market doesn't expect.

This is a pretty lofty approach to take, but there's nothing inherently wrong with this approach. Every time someone buys a stock, they are making a bet that they are getting a better deal because of something they see than the sorry schmuck who's selling them the stock.

Focusing your investments on sector funds allows you to invest in a basket of stocks in a particular geographic region or sector of the stock market. You're believing that you can get better returns than you could with the 500 index, or you simply want to diversify beyond that index. Here are reasons why you might want to invest in a sector fund:

- To diversify internationally in markets outside the United States.
- To invest in emerging markets, such as Brazil, China, Hong Kong, and India.
- To invest in sectors of the economy you believe will grow rapidly.

A few specific examples

Let's just take a look at a few specific examples of ways you can use index funds to focus your investing:[1]

NINETEEN
PORTFOLIO #1

Portfolio #1

- 80% S&P 500 Index Fund
- 10% Short-Term Treasury Index Fund
- 10% International Stock Index Fund

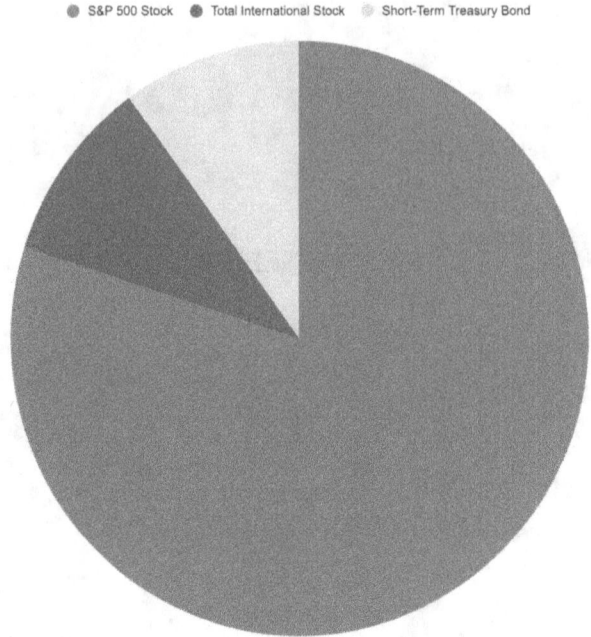

80% S&P 500 Index Fund, 10% Short-Term Treasury Fund, and 10% International Stock Fund.

THIS PORTFOLIO ADDS to the simple portfolio presented in Chapter 6. The only difference you will see here is the additio of Vanguard Total International Stock Index Fund (VTIAX).

This index fund provides excellent exposure to international stocks which could be especially useful for an investor who already owns the S&P 500 Index Fund and wants to invest in companies outside the United States.

Vanguard Total International Stock Index Fund invests in about 7,440 different stocks outside of the US, and there are a wide range of companies included in it from developed countries like France, Germany, Norway, Sweden, Switzerland, the UK, and Japan to emerging market countries, such as Brazil, China, India, Russia. and Taiwan.

With this one fund you get instant exposure to stocks in countries whose companies may be growing faster than those in the US. You may also find that the stocks in other countries have lower valuations than stocks in the US.

TWENTY
PORTFOLIO #2

Portfolio #2

- 70% S&P 500 Index Fund
- 10% Short-Term Treasury Index Fund
- 10% International Stock Index Fund
- 10% Emerging Markets Index Fund

THIS PORTFOLIO PROVIDES MORE exposure to emerging market stocks than you'd get with Portfolio #1.

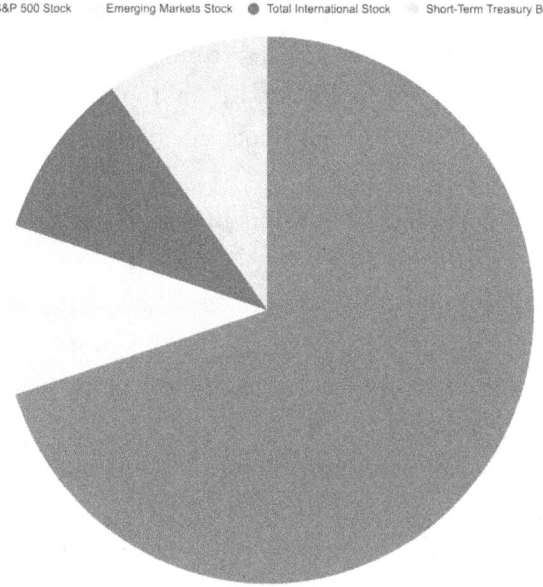

70% S&P 500 Index Fund, 10% Short-Term Treasury Fund, 10% International Stock Fund, and 10% Emerging Markets Stock Fund.

By adding the Vanguard Emerging Markets Stock Index you will have more exposure to companies in Hong Kong, Taiwan, China, India, and Brazil.

I Like Emerging Markets

I happen to like investing in emerging markets stocks, simply because I think they have cheaper valuations than stocks in the US. These emerging countries are like the wild teenagers of the investing world. They have a lot of potential but aren't very predictable!

I think emerging market stocks—especially those in China—represent enormous opportunities for the long-term investor. Charlie Munger recently said, "The best companies in China are cheaper than the best companies in the United States,[1]" and I agree with him completely.

Munger invests his family's wealth in Berkshire Hathaway, Costco, and with a Chinese Hedge fund manager named Li Lu. Munger began investing with Li Lu in the mid-2000s. Munger explained why this investor has appealed to him in a way no others have in nearly a century.

"He's partly a Chinese Warren Buffett. That really helps," he said. "Partly he's fishing in China. Not in this over-searched, over-populated, highly competitive American market."[2]

I like emerging market index funds because I want to participate in the growth of companies in Brazil, China, Hong Kong, India and other emerging markets.

Portfolio #2 gives you more exposure to emerging markets index funds. I think that if you're an investor you might like the additional exposure to Asian markets that you can get from holding some shares of an emerging markets index fund.

Vanguard's Emerging Markets Index Fund

Let's dive deep into Vanguard's Emerging Markets Index Fund (VEMAX) so that you can see some more details about how the fund invests shareholder money. This fund allocates investments in stocks based in these countries:

Hong Kong: 23.41%
Taiwan: 14.45%
China: 11.84%
India: 10.74%
Brazil: 8.37%
South Africa: 5.30%
Russian Federation: 4.04%
Thailand: 3.87%
Mexico: 2.88%
Malaysia: 2.81%

I think it's incredible that you can invest in *emerging markets stocks* at a low cost. Through this one fund, your investment is spread across 5,074 different stocks.[3]

As an investor, I don't have a crystal ball nor do I know if Alibaba or Tencent will be successful 10 or 20 years from now. But I don't have to worry about those individual companies when I buy shares in this fund. I do well if companies in those geographic areas of the world do well.[4]

Month-end 10 largest holdings

(21.00% of total net assets) as of 11/30/2019

1. Alibaba Group Holding Ltd.: 4.90%
2. Taiwan Semiconductor Manufacturing Co. Ltd.: 4.30%
3. Tencent Holdings Ltd.: 4.20%
4. China Construction Bank Corp.: 1.30%
5. Ping An Insurance Group Co. of China Ltd.: 1.20%
6. Reliance Industries Ltd.: 1.20%
7. Naspers Ltd.: 1.10%
8. Industrial & Commercial Bank of China Ltd.: 1.00%
9. Housing Development Finance Corp. Ltd.: 1.00%
10. Petroleo Brasileiro SA: 0.80%

TWENTY-ONE
PORTFOLIO #3

Portfolio #3

- 60% S&P 500 Index Fund
- 10% Short-Term Treasury Index Fund
- 10% International Stock Index Fund
- 10% Emerging Markets Index Fund
- 10% Small-Cap Index Fund

THIS PORTFOLIO PROVIDES exposure to small-cap stocks based in the United States that you don't get with Portfolio #2.

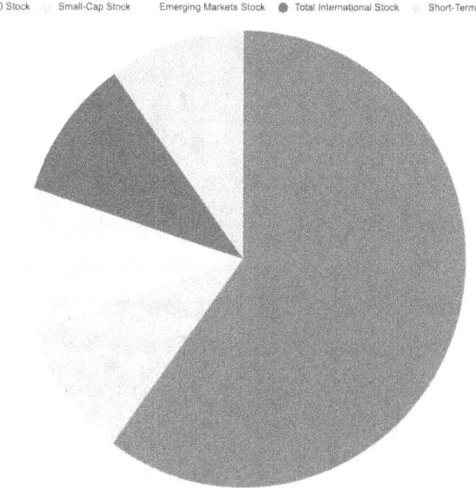

60% S&P 500 Index Fund, 10% Short-Term Treasury Index Fund, 10% International Index Fund, 10% Emerging Market Index Fund and 10% Small-Cap Index Fund.

This allocation simply adds a small-cap index fund to the previous portfolio. Why would an investor want to do this? Well, smaller companies have a history of growing faster than large companies. Makes sense, right? If you're small you can double in size, and double again, and this is easier to do if you're a $7 billion company than if you're a $700 billion company. In fact, what you really want to do is buy the $7 billion companies before they become $700 billion giants.

That's the idea behind buying small-cap stocks, but investing in small companies is risky if you buy individual stocks, because some small companies double, while others halve or disappear entirely.

A small-cap stock index that invests in 1,373 of these companies is useful because you get the benefit of the asset class without company-specific risk; you won't even notice if a few of these small companies fail. Small companies might grow faster than larger companies because it's easier to grow when you start small. If this idea appeals to you then you can add a small company index fund to your portfolio.

As you can see in this portfolio, your investments are in both large and small companies based in the United States and other countries. The four funds hold more than 5,000 stocks combined, which gives you a high degree of diversification and exposure to different countries around the world.

International Stocks are not Required

You should know that even though we're talking about international index funds in this chapter, you don't have to invest in them. They are not required if you want to be an excellent investor. You can do just fine by sticking with the stocks of companies based in the US.

I like to invest internationally because I believe that the United States stock market is heavily analyzed and picked over, so there aren't really cheap stocks and valuations seem "high" compared to alternatives in other developed countries or emerging market countries, like Brazil, China, or India.

I like international and emerging market funds because they let me buy stocks that I think are cheaper and have greater growth potential over the next few decades.

If you take anything with you at all from this section, I hope you'll remember the following:

1. For a first investment, consider a 500 index as your foundation.
2. Diversify with international index funds, emerging market funds, or both.
3. Consider sector funds[1] if you want to invest in specific parts of the market.

TWENTY-TWO

CHOCOLATE, VANILLA, OR SWIRL?

IF THE S&P 500 Index Fund is vanilla, and the Vanguard International Index Fund is chocolate, then you can think of a total world index as swirl.

A world index fund combines the stocks of companies in the United States with stocks from companies around the world; the *Vanguard Total World Stock Index Fund* (VTWAX) invests in 8,232 stocks from around the world.

Countries represented in the Vanguard Total World Stock Fund:[1]

United States
Japan
United Kingdom
China
Canada
France
Switzerland
Germany
Australia

Taiwan
Korea
Hong Kong
India
Netherlands
Brazil
Sweden
Italy
Spain
South Africa
Denmark
Finland
Russia
Singapore
Thailand
Belgium

The percentage of each country in the fund:[2]

United States: 55.7%
Japan: 7.7%
United Kingdom: 5.0%
China: 3.5%
Switzerland: 2.60%
Germany: 2.5%
Australia: 2.2%
Taiwan: 1.51%

Here are the fund's top holdings:[3]

1. Apple Inc.: 2.20%
2. Microsoft Corporation: 2.10%
3. Alphabet: 1.40%
4. Amazon Inc: 1.30%
5. Facebook Inc: 0.84%
6. Berkshire Hathaway: 0.80%

7. JPMorgan Chase & Co.: 0.80%
8. Johnson & Johnson: 0.64%
9. Visa Inc. Class A: 0.58%
10. Procter & Gamble Co.: 0.50%

This fund has a low expense ratio of .09% and has 8,232 holdings,[4] which provides far greater diversification than the S&P 500 index alone. This fund invests in small, mid, and large-cap stocks, providing exposure to companies of all sizes, not just the large-cap stocks held in the S&P 500.

As you can see, the fund's top holdings mirror the S&P 500 Index because the weighting is biased toward large companies in the United States.

This fund owns positions in Nestle, Tencent, Roche, Novartis, Toyota, HSBC, Samsung, and thousands of other international companies.

For someone who wants to mainly own stocks of US companies but also own international stocks, this offers a very low-cost way to achieve it with one fund.

My personal preference is to buy a 500 index and separate funds for international and emerging markets funds because I like to determine the allocation among funds myself.

There are infinite ways to change your allocation among sectors, but one, two, or three funds are more than enough for a well-diversified portfolio.

How to simplify with total world index funds.

1. A total world index fund provides wide diversification across 8,232 companies of all sizes across the world.
2. Total world index funds provide a simple and diversified way to invest in companies in the United States and internationally with one simple investment.

3. These mutual funds may be useful for investors who would like exposure to economies beyond the United States using only one index fund.

TWENTY-THREE

SECTOR FUNDS

Sector Funds Give Focus

FOR THOSE WHO would like to invest in specific business sectors or geographic regions, sector funds make a lot of sense; they let you own a collection of stocks and they greatly decrease company-specific risk.

Sector index funds let you invest with precision. You can invest in stocks from specific countries or industry sectors.

Many sector index funds have higher minimum initial investments than ETFs. For example, in order to invest in the Vanguard Health Care Fund (VGHCX) the minimum initial investment is $3,000.

Almost all index funds have corresponding ETFs that you can buy for the price of a single share. For example, you can buy a share of the Vanguard Health Care ETF (VHT) for $192.63 (as of 1/24/2020), which might be more reasonable for an investor just getting started.

A Solid Emerging Market Fund

I'll tell you why I like and own the Vanguard Emerging Markets Index Fund (VEMAX), which has an equivalent ETF (VWO).

I like this fund because it invests emerging market stocks of companies from around the world. This is useful to me because I'd like to invest in Chinese companies, like Alibaba and Tencent, but I don't understand Chinese companies well enough to invest in any one of those stocks.

The Vanguard Emerging Markets Index and ETF invests in many *emerging market stocks* at low cost. With one share of the fund an investor owns a part of 5,074 different stocks[1] in companies in China, Taiwan, Hong Kong, India, Brazil, and many others.

You benefit if these emerging markets companies grow, but you're not harmed by the failure of any one stock. I think this is an exceptional option for investors who want to participate in the growth of China's economy, but don't feel capable of picking stocks from Chinese companies.

The Top 10 holdings of Vanguard Emerging Markets Index Fund (VEMAX) and ETF (VWO):[2]

1. Alibaba Group Holding (China): 5.80%
2. Tencent Holdings (Hong Kong): 4.40%
3. Taiwan Semiconductor Manufacturing Co. (Taiwan): 4.30%
4. China Construction Bank Corp. (China): 1.30%
5. Ping An Insurance Group Co. (China): 1.20%
6. Naspers Ltd. (South Africa): 1.10%
7. Reliance Industries (India): 1.10%
8. Industrial & Commercial Bank of China (China): 1.00%
9. Petroleo Brasileiro (Brazil): 0.90%
10. Housing Development Finance Corp. (India): 0.90%

Okay, you might be thinking that investing in Brazil, China, and India is risky, and sure, there are risks involved in emerging markets. I realize that and accept the risks. In my view, the stocks in these countries have better valuations than comparable companies in the United States.

Vanguard Developed Markets Index Fund

The Vanguard FTSE Developed Markets Index Fund is an international index fund is a sensible choice for those who want to invest internationally, but prefer not to invest in emerging markets. These funds invest in companies based in countries with more developed legal systems that protect intellectual property. Developed countries like the United States recognize intellectual property, and this is important to investors because it helps to protect a company's intellectual property.

Why is a country's recognition of intellectual property so important to an investor? Software companies like Adobe and Microsoft develop Photoshop and Word, respectively, and they make money by selling licenses to their software. Now, if you invest in the stock of a company in an emerging market like China, that country may not recognize intellectual property.

An emerging market company could make it difficult for a company to protect its trademarks or copyrights, or they might not have laws that prevent piracy or counterfeit products. The lack of laws can make it difficult for a business to make a profit. Therefore, investing in emerging markets may have more risks, but investing in developed markets generally offer greater protection due to laws and regulations set up to protect the rights of businesses and entrepreneurs.

I like this fund a lot because the Vanguard FTSE Developed Markets Index Fund ETF invests in companies based in the developed and stable economies of countries like Canada, South Korea, and Switzerland.

The top three holdings of the Vanguard FTSE Developed Markets Index Fund (VTMGX) and ETF (VEA) as of 12/31/2019:[3]

1. Nestle SA (Switzerland): 1.60%
2. Samsung Electronics Co. (South Korea): 1.30%
3. Royal Dutch Shell (Netherlands): 1.20%
4. Roche Holding (Switzerland): 1.20%
5. Novartis (Switzerland): 1.00%
6. Toyota Motor Corp. (Japan): 0.90%
7. HSBC Holdings (Hong Kong): 0.80%
8. Unilever (London): 0.70%
9. TOTAL (France): 0.70%
10. AstraZeneca (UK): 0.70%

Sector Funds for Health Care Investing

If you want to harness the power of the healthcare sector, for example, but don't know which stock to buy, Vanguard's Health Care ETF (VHT) gives you exposure to stocks[4] from Johnson & Johnson, Pfizer, Medtronic, Amgen, AbbVie, Bristol-Myers Squibb, and 397 others.

If I wanted to invest in this part of the market—because I thought it had better growth prospects than another part or because I thought these stocks were cheap—then I could access them through this ETF.

Sector Funds for Biotech Investing

I don't invest in biotech stocks for the simple fact that they seem extremely risky. But there is one company that has interested me for the last year, Exact Sciences Corporation (EXAS), a molecular diagnostics company with an initial focus on the early detection and prevention of colorectal cancer. They have a specialized test that helps detect colon cancer, and if it works and gets approved by the FDA, the company could become insanely valuable. Imagine a test that saves money and saves lives. But the problem with biotech investing is if the company develops one drug and doesn't pass FDA testing, the stock can become worthless.

So rather than invest in exact sciences, you can invest in a fund like the SPDR S&P Biotech ETF (XBI), which invests in a basket of 123 stocks that also include:[5]

1. Invitae Corp.: 1.96%
2. BioMarin Pharmaceutical Inc.: 1.93%
3. Vertex Pharmaceuticals Inc.: 1.91%
4. Exact Sciences Corporation: 1.87%
5. United Therapeutics Corporation: 1.87%
6. Exelixis, Inc.: 1.81%
7. Seattle Genetics Inc.: 1.79%
8. Gilead Sciences Inc.: 1.76%
9. Alnylam Pharmaceuticals Inc.: 1.75%
10. Alexion Pharmaceuticals Inc.: 1.74%

I personally don't feel the need to invest in biotech stocks, because they're outside my circle of competence, but for those who do understand this niche and want to invest, it seems to be a good way to gain exposure to the sector without risking a lot in any one stock.

Even the largest holdings are less than 2%, so your downside related to any one stock is reduced. If I wanted to invest in biotech stocks, this would be more attractive than investing in any one risky biotech stock.

Sector Funds for Small-Cap Investing

The Vanguard Small-Cap Index Fund Admiral Shares (VSMAX) has a reasonable minimum initial investment of $3,000, but you can buy shares of the same fund through the VB ETF for the price of one share.

I like the way a fund like this lets you invest and get the returns of small-cap stocks without having to invest in specific small-cap stocks. I've researched several small-cap stocks and my current level of understanding would still make it a bit of a gamble for me.

For an investor who doesn't have the time or desire to invest in small-cap stocks directly, this Vanguard index fund makes this universe easily accessible. For a low cost, you can invest in 1,361 different stocks. As you can see below, even the largest holdings are about a third of one percent so you're not in trouble if one or a few go out of business.

1. Leidos Holdings Inc.: 0.40%
2. Zebra Technologies Corp.: 0.40%
3. Atmos Energy Corp.: 0.30%
4. IDEX Corp.: 0.30%
5. STERIS PLC: 0.30%
6. Teledyne Technologies Inc.: 0.30%
7. Equity LifeStyle Properties Inc.: 0.30%
8. Tyler Technologies Inc.: 0.30%
9. Allegion plc: 0.30%
10. Teradyne Inc.: 0.30%

Sector Funds for Technology Investing

If I could go back in time 10 or 20 years I would back up the truck and load it with a ton of Vanguard Information Technology Index ETF (VGT), [6] because it holds the stocks of tech companies like Apple, Microsoft, and Adobe.

I like how instead of picking just one tech stock, your investment gets spread across 322 stocks.

The Vanguard Information Technology ETF (VGT) Fund's top 10 holdings:[7]

1. Apple Inc.: 18.50%
2. Microsoft Corp.: 16.00%

3. Visa Inc.: 4.20%
4. Mastercard Inc.: 3.80%
5. Intel Corp.: 3.70%
6. Cisco Systems Inc.: 2.90%
7. Adobe Inc.: 2.20%
8. NVIDIA Corp.: 1.90%
9. salesforce.com Inc.: 1.90%
10. Accenture PLC: 1.90%

My time machine would also give me the chance to buy shares of Vanguard Consumer Discretionary Index ETF (VCR),[8] which has Amazon, Nike, and Starbucks among its 10 largest holdings.

The Vanguard Discretionary Income Fund ETF (VCR)

Fund's top 10 holdings:[9]

1. Amazon.com Inc.: 22.80%
2. Home Depot Inc.: 7.40%
3. McDonald's Corp.: 4.60%
4. NIKE Inc.: 3.90%
5. Starbucks Corp.: 3.30%
6. Lowe's Cos. Inc.: 2.90%
7. Booking Holdings Inc.: 2.70%
8. TJX Cos. Inc.: 2.30%
9. Target Corp.: 2.00%
10. General Motors Co.: 1.40%

There's a strong attraction that draws us to stocks that have done well in the past. It may be because the companies they represent are truly amazing, or maybe their stock price has gone through the roof during the past decade.

Well, sometimes their stock performance changes, and it can happen on the turn of a dime. For example, tech stocks were on fire from around 1996 until 2000. They were the fastest growing sector of the stock market. Then tech stocks crashed. For a long time, people swore off tech stocks and invested in companies perceived as "safe".

Well, I'm not saying this will happen again, but just because Apple, Microsoft, Adobe, NVIDIA, Amazon, Salesforce, and Tesla are on a roll now does not mean that those sectors will be the top performers in the next decade.

The stocks that were good investments yesterday may not continue to outperform tomorrow. It seems to me like basic human psychology to project what worked in the past into the future, but sometimes things change dramatically. Some investors have been investing in the energy sector for years as the price of oil declines, and they're losing a lot of money. People who invested in the financial sector lost a ton during the financial crisis. Those who invested in airlines or cruise ships got crushed when the Coronavirus hit.

Keep in mind that any time you decide to put extra money into a sector fund you're exposing yourself to risk. Risk is not necessarily bad, because there's positive risk (your sector does well) but the negative risk is if things do poorly.

The funds below are all available as index funds with high minimum initial investments. You will see ETFs listed below simply because they are available starting at the price of one share, which will require a significantly lower minimum to invest than investing in an index fund.

For example, the minimum initial investment for the Vanguard Communication Services index (VTCAX) is $100,000. The ETF price per share as of June 5, 2020 is $96.49 which makes the ETF much more accessible to most investors.

Vanguard Sector & Specialty ETFs

- Communication Services (VOX)
- Consumer Discretionary (VCR)
- Consumer Staples (VDC)

- Energy (VDE)
- Financials (VFH)
- Health Care (VHT)
- Industrials (VIS)
- Information Technology (VGT)
- Materials (VAW)
- Real Estate (VNQ)
- Utilities (VPU)

Your success picking specific sector index funds depends on your ability to understand or predict which sectors will outperform in the future. Market forecasting is impossible to do reliably, but I don't think it would be a sin if there was a sector you believe will do well in the next decade or two for you to emphasize it with a sector fund rather than buy just one stock.

You and every other investor out there are trying to pick the winning stock, but that's hard to do consistently. And it comes with a steep downside if you're wrong. However, owning a broad swath of a particular sector removes the risk of picking one stock and being wrong.

This approach of optimizing your index fund mix is definitely for those who like to tweak their investments and try to get better results than the S&P. Yes, this can be done, but it's like fortunetelling.

Sector Funds Can Increase Your Risk

Sector funds can help you improve your returns compared to what you'd get with the S&P 500 Index Fund. If you bet that a certain sector will outperform the broad index *you can beat the market averages if you're right.*

However, *you can really screw things up if you're wrong.* For example, I invested money with an actively managed mutual fund many years ago (before I realized that index funds are superior) and I noticed in their last annual report that they invested more money in the energy sector because valuations for oil refining companies seemed dirt cheap. They essentially made a "bet" that these companies' shares were underpriced and would eventually move higher when investors realized the underlying value of the companies.

A few months later Saudi Arabia and Russia went into a battle over oil prices. Saudi Arabia lowered oil prices and increased oil production to flooded the market with oil and make it hard for Russia to sell oil profitably. Through its actions, Saudi Arabia was trying to drive Russia out of the oil business.

One the one hand this made oil and gas cheap for people who buy gas for their cars or use oil to hear their homes, but this action severely hurt oil refining companies in the United States. Occidental Petroleum and Hess Corporation (two of the mutual funds large investments) had their stock prices hammered, falling 20% to 30% in one day. Clearly this bet on the energy sector caused a huge financial loss to mutual fund investors if they sold their shares. Those (including me) who don't sell their mutual fund shares may be fortunate enough to see some of these energy stocks recover in the future.

The "take home" lesson here is that you assume extra risk when you make a bet on one particular sector. The risk could have a positive outcome if you're right and the sector has the wind at its back, but it could have a negative outcome if the sector faces strong headwinds like the energy sector in the example above.

Keep in mind that when you invest money into a specific sector and you are correct you can win big, but if that sector suffers you can lose a lot of money (if you sell your shares) due to factors beyond your control.

One more example is investors who bought a lot of airline stocks before the Coronavirus outbreak. Airlines like Alaska, Delta, JetBlue, Southwest and United saw their stock prices plummet 30% - 50% in one week when markets realized people would suddenly stop flying. If you had loaded up on the transportation sector you would have seen your portfolio value drop like a stone.

It seems to me that starting with a broad based large cap index fund like the S&P 500 Index Fund or ETF as a base, and then adding sector funds to accentuate your portfolio makes more sense than only investing in sector funds.

If you take anything with you at all from this section, I hope you'll remember the following:

- You can combine international or sector funds with your 500 index.
- You can invest using index funds focused on international stocks, specific sectors of the economy, and companies of various sizes.
- Sector funds reduce "company specific risk" while providing exposure to an entire business sector or geographic region.

TWENTY-FOUR
EXPLODING PIÑATA EXCITEMENT

THE MOST SURPRISING thing about index funds and ETF investing is that you can beat the professional investors.

That's because you can buy a part of Apple, Microsoft, Amazon, Google, Facebook, Berkshire Hathaway, Adobe, Mastercard, Intel, Procter & Gamble and hundreds of other companies all at once in one low-cost index fund.

That's exciting!

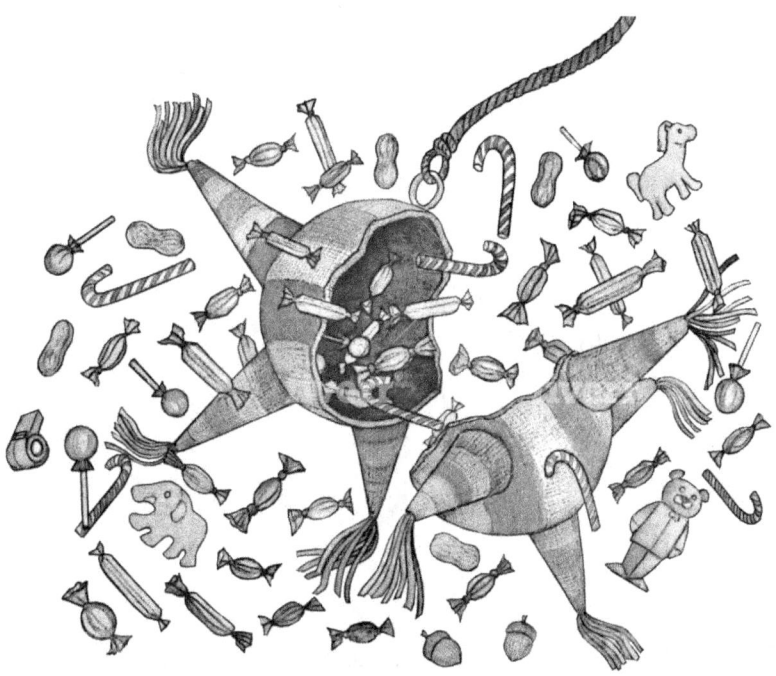

Index funds are as exciting as a piñata exploding with candy. A single index fund is made up of many different companies, and you can own them all in one investment. Illustration by Edwin Yaguar Chávez

TWENTY-FIVE
EXCITING LIKE FEDERER PLAYS TENNIS

LET'S look at the combination of qualities that make Roger Federer able to perform at such a high level for so many years. I would argue that these exact qualities are what also set index funds apart.

Here are five qualities that set Federer apart. Other players possess some of these qualities, but he has them all.

1. Federer is *efficient*: His biomechanics and fluidity are out of this world. They make him so light on his feet that Federer seems to float effortlessly across the court. His career has been lengthened by frictionless play.
2. Federer hits with *power*: His forehand and serve are among the best in the game. His mechanics let him hit the ball cleanly, without wasting energy and getting tired.
3. Federer is *precise*: He is the best server in tennis because of his control and ability to serve the ball to almost any location. His backhand slice is an especially effective weapon because he gets angles no-one else can.
4. Federer plays *attacking tennis*: His whole game is based

on setting up his forehand, which he can hit with confidence and power.
5. Federer is *relaxed*: If you watch him play, he's never out of breath. He never looks tense, and he has the ability to stay calm and relaxed under pressure. This has enabled him to remain poised in high pressure points.

Similarly, index funds provide an efficient, powerful, and precise way to attack the market while allowing you to sit back and relax.

- ***Index funds & ETFs are efficient***: Their low costs and infrequent trading make them tax efficient. They deliver the markets' return without excessive expenses, fees, or taxes.
- ***Index funds & ETFs give you power***: They harness the power of stock ownership of the largest companies in the United States.
- ***Index funds & ETFs are precise***: Investors can buy stocks in US companies, they can invest internationally, or they can select index funds that invest in specific market sectors.
- ***Index funds & ETFs let you attack***: Sector funds let investors attack specific areas of the stock market to concentrate their best ideas; for example tech, financials, healthcare, or energy.
- ***Index funds & ETFs let you relax***: You can relax knowing that you're not trying too hard to pick the right stocks and you won't be hurt if one stock in the fund performs poorly. Index funds & ETFs give peace of mind through diversification.

If you take anything with you at all from this section, I hope you'll remember the following:

- Index funds and ETFs are efficient, powerful, and precise
- Index finds and ETFs combine diversification and rock-bottom costs
- Index funds and ETFs perform better than most funds run by highly paid investment managers

PART THREE
INTELLIGENT STOCK INVESTING

TWENTY-SIX

WHY PICK STOCKS?

EVEN THOUGH THIS book is about index investing, I'm including a section about stocks. You might be asking yourself, "Why the hell would you teach people about picking stocks when the bulk of the book says you probably can't beat the market?"

We know it's hard to beat the 500 index, but some people just want to buy stocks. No matter what you say, they will still want to try.

TWENTY-SEVEN
KIDS ARE GONNA PARTY

PARENTS WHO HAVE teenagers getting ready to go to a party might give advice like "Don't drink, don't do drugs," etc. We've all been there. But despite what our parents tell us, most kids are gonna experiment with forbidden fruit anyways. Peer pressure and curiosity always win the day.

The same can be said about investing. I can write about index funds being good for most people, but some curious and energetic investors are going to want to buy stocks. I don't blame people who want to buy stocks. The phone apps have amazing visualizations, and trading is now free. You add the potential to get rich quick, and who wouldn't want to give it a try?

Rather than tell teens to avoid all of the things that surround young people at school and parties: drinking, drugs, sex, you name it, parents are better off educating their kids ahead of time. By the same token, I know some readers will want to experiment with stocks, and I want them to be prepared.

TWENTY-EIGHT

INVESTING VS. GAMBLING

WHEN YOU INVEST money into a business that you understand for the long term and have a reasonable expectation of a return, then you're investing.

If you're more into gambling, you can go on Robinhood and hack some shit to get paper for chicken tendies. But that's not a strategy for long-term success (though it might make you a hero on Wall Street Bets)[1].

Here, sadly, we're going to focus on investing instead of gambling. In his book "One Up On Wall Street,"[2] Peter Lynch said, "To me, an investment is simply a gamble in which you've managed to tilt the odds in your favor." I think Lynch has a terrific view—it doesn't matter whether it's Las Vegas, the S&P 500, or Bitcoin.

TWENTY-NINE

ASKING SIMPLE QUESTIONS

ASK simple questions about companies to learn which ones are likely to grow and which will probably fail. You can compare investing with poker, as Lynch points out:

"You can never be certain what will happen, but each new occurrence—a jump in earnings, the sale of an unprofitable subsidiary, the expansion into new markets—is like turning up another card. As long as the cards suggest favorable odds of success, you stay in the hand."

If you like the retail sector, you have to start figuring out which companies are succeeding and which are failing. It's obvious that Amazon has disrupted the entire sector, but it appears that some companies are finding unique ways to try and compete, and some are succeeding.

As of this writing, it looks like Target, Costco, and Walmart are adapting well, and Macy's, JC Penny, and Sears are roadkill. In addition to retail success, Amazon is killing it with cloud computing (AWS) and the AI-powered Alexa devices. Every new occurrence in Amazon's business, like buying Whole Foods, gives investors another idea of what can happen in the future.

Your success as a stock investor depends on your ability to find stocks in companies that continue to innovate, improve their brands, and strengthen their bond with customers. Tesla is an example of a company that has been doing all three successfully, as wild as the ride may be for investors.

You will become a better investor when you start identifying the winners and losers as early in the game as possible.

THIRTY

I LIKE STOCKS

ALTHOUGH I OWN index funds and like them enough to write a whole book about them, *I like stocks.* You may wonder how I can like both, because the start of this book discusses the benefits of index funds and says how hard it is to beat the market.

In my early days, I invested in index funds and then I slipped up and made a couple of bad stock investments. In the words of Mae West, "I used to be Snow White, but I drifted." So here I am now, writing you in 2020 after I started invested in the 500 index again so that I could "eat my own cooking."

I like having a foundation of index funds, and from there I can add stocks of companies that I believe offer the chance to outperform.

THIRTY-ONE
WHY EVEN BOTHER?

IF WE'VE ALREADY ESTABLISHED that most professionals can't beat the S&P, why should we even try? Well, because it's possible you could be better than the average investor. You'll never know if you don't try.

I see nothing wrong with investing in stocks with a small part of your investible money when you're getting started. I'd say start with index funds and once you have a nice foundation, then you can concentrate on individual stocks, which is how I started investing.

When I start learning about a company, and start figuring out what their products do, and how they compete against other companies, something just lights up in my brain.

THIRTY-TWO

GOOD WAYS TO GAIN UNDERSTANDING

I COULD MAKE this more complex, but long lists aren't going to help you. Temperament part is within your control. I can help you to learn more effectively, and that will help you with finding the stocks you understand.

A very useful tool to start with is the Value Line survey. You can type in a stock's ticker symbol to access a company report.

My library has a subscription to the Value Line database, so anyone with a library card can access it for free. If your library offers this service, I highly recommend using it. Otherwise, consider subscribing on the Value Line website.

Value Line offers grades of 1-5 (1 being best) for factors like "Safety" and "Timeliness". There's also a letter grade for "Financial Strength." The summaries provide useful information about the company and its strength within its sector, as well as the analyst's opinion on whether it's a sensible investment.

Value Line is a good place to get a "bird's eye view" and find out if you want to investigate a company further. I also highly recommend doing a quick Google search for the company's annual report.

This free document will teach you a lot about the company and what some of the highs and lows have been during the past year.

Annual reports are essential reading. Start with the shareholder letter and just read through it. Don't be intimidated and don't worry if you don't understand everything the first time you read it. You will get better at reading annual reports with time. After reading the shareholder letter, read the Form 10-K.

Value Line and reading the company's annual report are a good place to start learning about a company, and I also recommend taking an accounting course, or at least watching some YouTube videos to learn basic accounting concepts to figure out how to read the 10-K in the annual report.

If you take anything with you at all from this section, I hope you'll remember the following:

- Read Value Line Surveys to learn about stocks.
- Read annual reports to gain a deeper understanding.
- Study a business to become an expert before investing.

THIRTY-THREE

COME INTO YOUR OWN

IT IS essential to *come into your own*[1] as an investor. Even though you may admire your investing heroes or mentors, don't worry about what they might think; you must only buy the stocks that make sense to you.

"Part of the game of investing is to come into your own. You must find some way that perfectly fits your personality, because there is some element of a zero-sum game in investing. If you buy, somebody else has to sell. And when you sell, somebody has to buy. You can't both be right." Li Lu

I'll give you an idea of how ignoring these principles worked against me for several years and negatively affected my thinking. When I was just learning about investing I read everything I could about Warren Buffett's investing approach. You may know this already, but his strengths are analyzing banks, insurance companies, energy, furniture stores, building supplies, jewelry stores, Coke, McDonalds' GEICO, Dairy Queen, and railroads, among many others. Absent from this list are technology companies, because they have never fallen within his circle of competence.

As I grew up, I also avoided investing in tech companies, mainly because I used the same kind of "tech is too difficult for me to analyze" approach that Buffett employed for many years.[2] During the early 2000s I watched as companies like Amazon, Apple and Google were growing fast, but I never felt as though they were within my ability to understand. I know it sounds like I had blinders on, *because I did*. I automatically assumed that if a brilliant investor like Buffett can't understand Amazon, then I didn't stand a chance. This was a mistake—he was staying within his own circle of competence; he wasn't defining mine.

THIRTY-FOUR
COMING INTO MY OWN: AMAZON

I WANTED to buy Amazon stock for years, but I held back because of the rational thinking that the company seemed expensive and it was "undisciplined" of me to pay $500 a share.

Finally, at the end of 2017, I decided to buy stock in Amazon. It seemed expensive at the time, but I had to balance the valuation with the company's fast rate of innovation and success in many new areas of business.

I also knew that an investment in Amazon required belief in the company's future innovation. Bezos tells his employees that, "It's always day one," so Amazon acts like a startup and does not rely on what worked yesterday to solve today's problem. He believes the company can do that by obsessing about customers, focusing on results over process, and making high-quality decisions quickly.

The moment I committed to buying Amazon was when I came into my own as a better investor. I was not 100% certain I was making the right decision to buy the stock at its quoted price, but I was 70% sure and I didn't want to wait too long.

In the back of my mind, I was thinking, "A wise investor would never pay such a high price for this stock!" but I ignored that voice because I knew the company was innovating and growing. I even imagined that Warren Buffett might not have approved of my decision to buy Amazon at such a high price. Yet I kept true to my inner voice and that investment turned out to be one of my better ones.

Coming into your own by following your interests as an investor will help you learn new skills. All good records are a mixture of skill and luck,[1] and since you can't control the latter you might as well work on the former.

THIRTY-FIVE

COMING INTO MY OWN: WATERS

I CAME across a company called Waters Corporation over 10 years ago. I was searching for companies that had both a durable competitive advantage and talented leadership: Waters had both.

The company was especially interesting to me because of its involvement in the scientific instrument field, and I have a particular interest in this because I majored in biology and took a bunch of biology and chemistry classes that I really loved.

After doing some research about the company, I found that Waters is like the Apple of the scientific instrument world. There are many scientific measuring device companies out there — some of which make similar devices, but Waters makes the best machines, and the researchers who use them stay loyal to them for years. In other words, there's a stickiness when it comes to Waters' products.

One other thing that I appreciate about this company is that they sell the "picks and shovels" of the pharmaceutical, food safety, and academic markets. There's a lot of speculation involved in biotech companies given the regulatory hurdles and chances of failure. Waters provides tools to a variety of these companies, but it is not dependent on any specific drugs getting approved. Their tools are used to make sure that drugs are pure—that whatever makes it through the production process is 100% what it's supposed to be—and they're also used in testing food and water for safety and purity.

I used intuition to make this investment because I don't know any analysts who know about Waters, and I had no way of understanding the business beyond what I saw on their website and what I read in its annual report. But everything supported my understanding that this company had a wide economic moat (its intellectual property and high-end machines) and exemplary leadership, which has been consistent for the past decade while the company's stock has outpaced the return of the S&P 500. My only mistake with Waters was not buying more.

THIRTY-SIX

COMING INTO MY OWN: CARMAX

I BOUGHT Carmax stock a decade ago. It was one of the first stocks I bought when I started learning how to truly understand companies before buying stock. One mistake I made was not buying enough Carmax after the stock turned out to be one of my best all-time investments. I made my first purchase, and I just sort of watched the company grow its profits and build stores all around the country.

I actually bought a Toyota from Carmax soon after I became a shareholder, and I drive it to this very day. I wanted to learn about the company firsthand, and thought one way to do so was to actually purchase a car. I found a car that matched my specs in their Sacramento location (they had not opened a location in the Seattle area at the time), and I found a cheap flight from Seattle to Sacramento. But I didn't know how to get from the airport to the car lot.

I asked the Carmax salesman about shuttle services or taxis from the airport to their lot, and he told me not to worry about it, he'd pick me up. At that moment I knew this company was doing things right when it came to serving their customers. This salesman didn't even know I owned a single share of stock; his motivation was to sell me a car, and make it as easy as possible. Mission accomplished.

Carmax has been growing rapidly for the past 10 years since I bought the stock. The stock doubled. Then it doubled again. It continues to grow: the last time I looked it was up 50% in 2019.

It's taken me years to learn how to follow my interests and come into my own as an investor. Let your curiosity guide you, and as long as you're interested and learning new things, you're on the right path.

THIRTY-SEVEN

HOW WILL YOU COME INTO YOUR OWN?

WHAT COMPANIES MATCH YOUR INTERESTS?

Since you're going to spend a lot of your time improving on anything you get good at, you might as well love what you do. Li Lu expresses this pursuit perfectly:

"The game of investing is a process of discovering who you are, what you're interested in, what you're good at, what you love to do, then magnifying that until you gain a sizable edge over all the other people."

If you take anything with you at all from this section, I hope you'll remember the following:

- Come into your own as an investor.
- Stick to what you're good at and love what you do.
- Don't worry about others' opinions. Trust your intuition and pursue what interests you.
- For you to be right and win in a trade, the person on the other side has to lose.

- Find your edge and magnify it so you can gain an edge over other people.

THIRTY-EIGHT
FIND FAT PITCHES

I'VE ALWAYS BEEN a firm believer in the notion that you have to act decisively when you see something you like. Warren Buffett compares buying stock in things you know with Ted Williams' philosophy on hitting. Williams was the last person to hit .400 and he claims his success was swinging only at balls in his "sweet spot."

In "The Science of Hitting" Williams divided the strike zone into 77 circles, each one representing the location of a pitch. He said that if he swung at pitches in his "best" circles he could hit for a high average, but swinging for pitches in the "worst" circles would reduce his chances at success.

WINVESTING   121

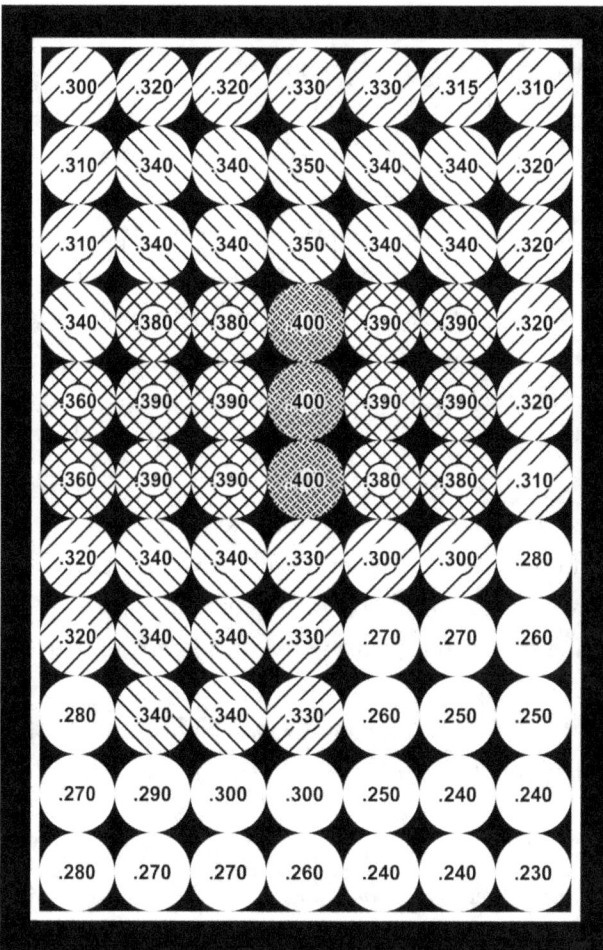

The strike zone divided into 77 circles, each representing a different pitch location in the batter's strike zone. The batting average is higher when a hitter swings at pitches they like. Similarly, an investor improves their chances for success when they buy stock they like and understand. Illustration by Advino.

Ted Williams had one problem that an investor doesn't have. If the pitcher threw a pitch in the strike zone, even if it wasn't in his sweet spot, he could get called out on strikes if he didn't swing. He'd have people yelling "Swing, you bum!" and sometimes he would be forced to swing at sub-optimal pitches.

But with investing you can wait for just the pitch you want, and there is absolutely no penalty for waiting. The stock market can offer you Apple at $299 or Amazon at $1,900 and you can just wait until you see the stock you like at the price you want to pay.

A good exercise is to write down your 25 best stock ideas. That may seem like a lot at first, but you'll hit that number quickly when you're reading and learning about a lot of different companies.

Next, circle the top five and cross out the rest. You have to say "no" and eliminate a lot of pretty good ideas to focus on your best ones and improve your batting average.

No one can really understand 25 companies that well. Even if you studied them all for hours on end, it would be far better to put more money into your third best idea than your 25th.

Just make sure you're waiting for fat pitches in your sweet spot. Li Lu put it this way:

"As a securities investor, you can watch all sorts of business propositions in the form of security prices thrown at you all the time. For the most part, you don't have to do a thing other than be amused. Once in a while, you will find a 'fat pitch' that is slow, straight, and right in the middle of your sweet spot. Then you swing hard. This way, no matter what natural ability you start with, you will substantially increase your hitting average."

Li Lu also points to one common problem amongst investors: they swing too often. However, the opposite problem is equally harmful to long-term results "You discover a 'fat pitch' but are unable to swing with the full weight of your capital,"[1] Li said.

If you take anything with you at all from this section, I hope you'll remember the following:

- Find your investing "sweet spot" where you have an advantage.
- Start with 25 stock ideas and eliminate 20 of them. Focus on five stocks you understand well.
- Say "no" most of the time.

THIRTY-NINE
BECOME MORE PRODUCTIVE

I SAW this amazing video of Scott Wadsworth, a craftsman featured in a YouTube video. In the video he provides spoken narration to a video showing him building a ramp that leads to his mother's home. He offers commentary about craftsmanship that's imbued with his philosophy on hard work and life.

There's nothing you can do that is smarter than learning from the people around you. One of C.S. Lewis' quotes is useful to keep in mind as a warning: "Two of a trade never agree."

Wadsworth says that two people who spend their lives doing the same type of work are never going agree that the other person's method is anywhere as good as theirs because, "That's the way I do it, therefore it's superior."

"The smartest thing we can do is decide before we ever get to work in the morning that everybody we meet that day is gonna have something that I can learn from them if I wanna learn it. This axiom has the bonus of being true in all cases. So the best thing you can do if you wanna become a

> more productive hand, if you want to experience the joy of getting more work done in a day than anyone thought was humanly possible — is make it a point to learn something from everyone around you ever day."[1]
>
> SCOTT WADSWORTH

Wadsworth speaks to the craftsmanship of building a house, or a ramp, or cutting wood efficiently, but you can apply this principle of learning from others to your investment learning.

The best way to become a better investor is by learning not just about stocks but a variety of different subjects. I read essays and books and watch videos about scientists and business leaders to try and learn important principles beyond the financial world. I feel that if you learn different subjects and arrange your learning in your head you can use the ideas for the rest of your life.

For example, several years ago I read a book by Robert Cialdini called "Influence,"[2] which is about the psychology of persuasion. The principles of that book have been useful to me in so many ways: they've helped me as a photographer, as a businessman, and with life's daily negotiations. That one book has been such a boon, and I try to keep reading books on the subjects I know nothing about so that I can become a more well-rounded person.

So, my advice to you is to read (or watch YouTube videos) about the big ideas outside of finance–engineering, physics, history, philosophy, psychology–and apply them to new situations and problems you face in life and your investing decisions. It's hard for me to tell you exactly how your learning will benefit you in the future, so you just have to take my word on it. You will be trying to make a decision between seven different stocks and one will just jump out at you because all of your learning will coalesce to make the wise choice that is obvious to you.

Munger says that if you commit yourself to lifelong learning, "I solemnly promise you that one day you'll be walking down the street and you'll look to your right and left and think, 'My heavenly days! I'm now one of the few most competent people of my whole age cohort.'"[3]

Wadsworth echoes Munger's sentiment about getting smart by learning and producing good work:

> "You will add that to your repertoire of tricks and techniques and after a while, not only will you be working harder—but you're gonna be smart. And people are gonna wonder: 'Wow. How did you learn all that stuff?' And you won't feel like you have to mention that it was all learned by keeping your eyes open while you were earning your living producing good work."
>
> SCOTT WADSWORTH

FORTY

INVESTING TOOLS: STOCK PUNCH CARD

LOU SIMPSON, who once invested in stocks for GEICO, and who Warren Buffett considers one of the worlds' best investors, was asked to describe his investment philosophy. "The essence is simplicity," he said.

"The more you trade," Simpson said, "the harder it is to add value because you're absorbing a lot of transaction costs, not to mention taxes."

Simpson said, "What we do is run a long-time-horizon portfolio comprised of ten to fifteen stocks."[1]

Diversifying is good if you're a know-nothing investor and are happy just owning an index fund, but once you've committed to beating the market averages, diversification makes no sense; once you buy a large number of stocks, you've created your own index fund.

The way extraordinary investors beat the market is through concentration. Most only own between three and 15 stocks. For example, Charlie Munger has his family's money in only three investments: Berkshire Hathaway, Costco, and Li Lu's fund, which invests in Chinese companies.

Some people might ask why these investors concentrate on their best ideas — but the opposite question is better: "Why *can't* you concentrate on your best ideas?"

If you buy many stocks, you lose focus on a few of your best ideas. If you have three or five great stock ideas, why on earth would you add your 30th best idea? To prevent yourself from buying too many stocks and improve the odds you truly understand the stocks you buy, Warren Buffett suggests that you have a stock "punch card".

STOCK MARKET INTELLIGENCE

LIFETIME STOCK PUNCH CARD

○ 1. _____   ○ 11. _____
○ 2. _____   ○ 12. _____
○ 3. _____   ○ 13. _____
○ 4. _____   ○ 14. _____
○ 5. _____   ○ 15. _____
○ 6. _____   ○ 16. _____
○ 7. _____   ○ 17. _____
○ 8. _____   ○ 18. _____
○ 9. _____   ○ 19. _____
○ 10. _____   ○ 20. _____

A stock punch card with 20 punches representing all the investments that you got to make in a lifetime. Once you'd punched through the card, you couldn't make any more investments at all. If you follow these rules you'll think really carefully about each stock and load up on what you really understand — and you'll do much better.

"I could improve your ultimate financial welfare by giving you a ticket with only 20 slots in it — so that you had 20 punches representing all the investments that you got to make in a lifetime," Buffett said. "Once you'd punched through the card, you couldn't make any more investments at all.[2]"

"Under these rules, you'd think really carefully about what you did, and you'd be forced to load up on what you'd really thought about. So you'd do so much better," he said.

What is Buffett driving at here? Well, too many people just swipe and tap a few buttons on an app and soon become the owner of 30, 50 or 100 stocks that they bought without much thought. Maybe a friend told them about a stock, or they read an article online, or Cramer mentioned it on TV.

Yet many of these stocks people pick quickly are almost random picks based on hope, and the investor's long-term results wind up average at best. This is why most investors can't beat the S&P index—they're not concentrating on their best ideas because they don't take the time to understand businesses on a deep level.

To clarify this mindset, Simpson said, "You can only know so many companies. If you're managing 50 or 100 positions, the chances that you can add value are much, much lower." Therefore, the punch-card approach in thinking things through first and limiting your investment decisions makes sense to him.

FORTY-ONE

I ACCIDENTALLY SMASHED MY IPHONE

AFTER I ACCIDENTALLY CRUSHED MY iPhone I went to the Apple Store to get it replaced. I was pretty bummed at the stupid mishap (I broke up a dog fight and fell to the ground with my phone beneath me). The sales associate was upbeat and understanding, and after I bought the replacement phone he told me that he loves photography and wants to pursue it as a profession.

He also mentioned that he's 19 and I couldn't resist giving him encouragement to start investing while he's young. I told him about index funds, and here's the graph I would have showed him if I had it on me (maybe something I should consider doing).

Here's how a 19-year-old can expect their money to grow if he starts with $3,000 (the minimum to open a Vanguard S&P 500 Index Fund account) and contributes $200 a month earning 10% return until he retires.[1]

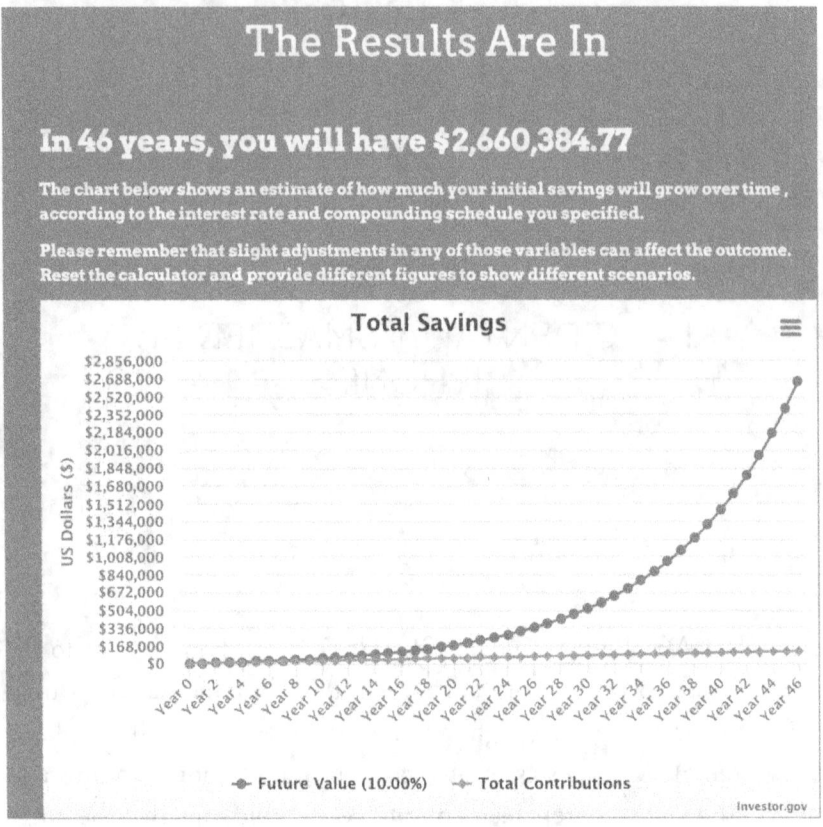

If you were to start investing with $3,000 and added $200 each month earning 10% the investment could be worth more than $2.5 million when you retire in 46 years. The actual rate of return will vary, yet this chart shows you how investing for the long term with index funds can provide you with remarkable investing returns.

It's also possible to accelerate the compound interest by socking away extra money. It's one of those simple things you can do to help yourself in life. It's a very easy habit to start.

By the way, it's possible to start investing in this mutual fund using an S&P 500 index fund ETF, and you don't have reach the minimum initial investment of $3,000. You can just buy one share of the Vanguard 500 ETF (ticker symbol VOO) for the price of a single share.

Just as acorns grow into mighty oaks, your investments will grow over time. You just have to plant that first seed to get started.

Peter Lynch observed that many investors "cut their flowers and water their weeds," meaning they sell their winners and keep their losers, hoping the losers will come back even. I have found his words to be on target in this regard. I've owned a few stocks I hoped would "bounce back" and they never did, while the wonderful companies just keep flowering.

For years I owned stock in a company called Leucadia National — it's since been renamed Jefferies Financial Group. I thought I understood the business and its leaders better than I actually did.[2] After the company's stock went nowhere for many years, I decided to sell my shares and reinvest the money in Amazon; it was the best investing decision I ever made.

FORTY-TWO
FLOWERS OF AMAZON

FOR YEARS I'd been watering the weeds of my Leucadia stock, and in one chop I severed the weeds of Leucadia and started watering the flowers of Amazon. I learned a valuable lesson from the Leucadia debacle, and I'll definitely be more alert to leadership changes and act swiftly whenever necessary – because I should have pressed the eject button from Leucadia years earlier.

Fortunately, I have never cut the flowers of my portfolio. I own shares of only four stocks: Amazon, Berkshire, Carmax, and Waters, and I don't plan to sell them any time soon. The best thing about great companies is that you can just sit on your ass while not making any decisions.

My four-stock portfolio is the result of using the punch-card approach and only considering a new stock if it's an improvement over what I already own. If not, I just pass. It's so damn simple.

FORTY-THREE

BIG THINGS START SMALL

AS AN INVESTOR, you need to think in the long term, which requires patience.

Jeff Bezos said that he has used this approach repeatedly at Amazon.[1] "We know from our past experiences that big things start small. The biggest oak starts from an acorn. You've got to be willing to let that acorn grow into a little sapling and then finally into a small tree, and maybe one day it will be a big business on its own."

If you take anything with you at all from this section, I hope you'll remember the following:

- Learn something from everyone you meet.
- Study the big ideas from as many disciplines as possible and apply them to the new situations and problems you face.
- Big things start small: Today's acorn becomes tomorrow's oak.

FORTY-FOUR
STEPPING IN RIVERS

THE GREEK PHILOSOPHER, Heraclitus, observed that a person cannot step in the same river twice because the person and the river change constantly. I'm reminded every day that an investor can't step twice in the same market because it changes constantly.

It's foolish that people think they can forecast the stock market.

They use feelings, emotions, and half-baked theories to predict the next market crash or recession. But it's total foolishness to try and predict the future when it's so hard because the economy and investing landscape are always changing.

Real-Life Example

"I'm 53 and just started investing 2 years ago. I'm going well with Old Man Dividend Stocks.

Hold Forever.

However I jumped in the stock market about 15 years ago and started to lose money quickly. I panicked and got out.

Boy to I regret that now.

I can only imagine what my portfolio would look like if I had a stronger stomach back then.

Damn It!!!!"

A YOUTUBE COMMENT

That is a perfect example of how investors shoot themselves in the foot. The stock market is there to serve you. This investor looked at the market, got spooked, and ran. That's the emotional response you don't want to have. It will ruin you and you will regret your decisions that are based on emotions.

But let's get this straight, I can't help you to not panic; an author can only do so much. I can, however, try to convince you that if you can stay calm under pressure then that equanimity will serve you well. I can also say that if you know that you tend to get scared with stock market uncertainty then you shouldn't invest.

And there's nothing wrong with that. In fact, it's better to know that ahead of time and not make mistakes after investing a boatload of your savings.

Stock Market Crashes

Stock market crashes are going to happen, but when they start, no one knows. If you're not ready for that, you shouldn't be in the stock market. I mean you have to be able to go about your life and not worry about the stock market. You need to separate your emotions from investing. The stomach is the key organ here. It's not the brain. Do you have the stomach for these kinds of declines? If your time horizon is 10 or 20 years then it shouldn't matter too much what happens in the next year or two, even if there's a market crash.

No One Knows When or Why

The most important point here is that no one knows when or why corrections happen. Investors are continually searching for reasons for stocks to fall. It almost becomes a game for some to say that the can predict the exact event that does it.

There's always something to fear that will possibly derail the market—low profit margins, valuations, earnings shortfalls, a recession, a global pandemic, the list goes on forever.

The problem is that sometimes stocks rise and fall for no apparent reason whatsoever. Occasionally these issues matter, but other times the market simply shrugs them off.

This past Thursday's 2% loss in the S&P 500 is a fine example of this. The headline writers tried to come up with the news of the day to explain why the market fell, but there wasn't much there. It's not always a neat and tidy explanation except for the fact that there are times when there's more selling pressure than buying pressure.

Folly of Market Timing

Peter Lynch said, "Far more money has been lost by investors preparing for corrections, or trying to anticipate corrections, than has been lost in corrections themselves.[1]"

Lynch has seen his share of crashes and explains why it's foolish to try and guess what's going to happen. "No one seems to know when they are gonna happen," Lynch said. "At least if they know about 'em, they're not telling anybody about 'em. I don't remember anybody predicting the market right more than once, and they predict a lot. So they're gonna happen.

If you're investing in stocks, to just have to be prepared that every couple of years the market will probably go down about 10%. Sometimes you will see the market decline 20%-30% and stay down for a while. "When they're gonna start, no one knows," Lynch said. "If *you're not ready for that, you shouldn't be in the stock market,"* he said. You need a strong stomach to survive a stock market crash. The stomach is the key organ, not the brain.

I like the image below, because it shows the relentless progress of the S&P 500 index over time. The gray areas are the recessions from 1930 to the present.

S&P 500 Index - 90 Year Historical Chart.

The stock market declined during those gray areas, often steeply. People panicked and sold, which caused the market to decline further. Yet the wise thing to do was to just stay put, not freak out, not try to predict the storm, and not try to time things perfectly.

I have survived three market crashes: the dot-com crash in 2000, the financial crisis of 2008, and the Coronavirus crash of 2020. I didn't sell a single stock or fund during any of those stock market crashes and I kept investing during these bear markets. The stock market has always recovered, and as you can see history shows the gradual movement up.

The experience of surviving three brutal stock market crashes taught me to keep extra cash safely stashed in a money market account at all times. You may not care a lot about boring cash when everything's going great, but when the market crashes you will be thankful you set something aside.

It helps to have cash after a crash because you don't have to see stocks you already own to pay near-term expenses, and having cash ready to deploy when the market crashes means you can invest when everyone's in a panic and stocks are cheap. If you're ever going to want to go on the offensive as an investor it will be when blood runs in the street, markets have dropped 1,000, 2,000, or 3,000 points or more[2] – that's when you get to buy great companies on sale. It's also easier not to panic when you realize your horizon is not one or two years, but ten or 20 years.

Why is Market Timing so Hard?

1. You have to decide when to sell your stocks
2. You have to decide when to get back in
3. You must time both decisions correctly

Can you see the problem there? It's very hard to do this correctly, and Peter Lynch comes to mind when thinking about how more money is lost by investors preparing or trying to anticipate corrections, than in the corrections themselves. The reason for this is if you do #1 correctly and sell all (or most of) your stocks, then you wind up waiting while the market climbs and you miss out on the market's return while waiting for the next recession to hit.

Missing Gains Waiting for Crashes

By the way, nobody is right about everything, and I may be wrong about this. So don't take my word as the final one. I think the best you can take from it is to look at the record of someone who got out of the stock market in 2017 and is waiting for the crash. How much gain was missed as they awaited the crash? Would their gain have been 75% or 100%? If so, wouldn't it have been worth it even if the losses were 30%, 40%, or even 50% in a market crash?

I personally just remain invested and don't try to predict crashes. I would rather build an ark than try to predict a flood.

. . .

If you take anything with you at all from this section, I hope you'll remember the following:

- Nobody can forecast the market
- Market timers are usually wrong
- Keep a long-term perspective

FORTY-FIVE
INTUITIVE INVESTING

What is Intuition?

INTUITION IS KNOWING WITHOUT KNOWING. It's going from A to Z without stopping at all the letters along the way.[1]

It's coming to a conclusion quickly without taking time at that moment to assess why you came to that conclusion.

Intuition is knowing something without knowing why. You can think of intuition as seeing the image before all the pieces of the puzzle are in place.

The reality is that logic is plodding, slow, and unoriginal. Logic spends valuable time thinking about the way things turn out to be, or used to be, or could be, or might be. In nature, an animal doesn't spend any time doing any of that. An animal threatened by another doesn't use logic; it uses intuition and instinct. What's the difference between the two?

Instinct is inbred: each animal is born with it. But intuition is a process that is constantly learning things. As we learn throughout our lives, we gain new distinctions about things, which then goes into our process. We slow down as we're driving by the car accident. And we look. Why? Because we're gaining a piece of information. "Ah, that intersection is blind. Ah, those small cars are dangerous. Ah, people drink and drive too much." Whatever it is you take away from that accident, you take it away for the purposes of your survival.[2]

The resource we use most frequently in Western culture is logic. If we think about something with the "conscious" part of our brain we engage logic. Yet, thinking alone can hold us back.

You know more than you think. In our modern society, intuition can help you gather resources to help you survive. You can use your intuition to find safe and productive investments. You don't have to throw logic and reason out the window, of course, but your intuition might be more powerful than logic.

So, the question you must ask is: *"How can I use intuition to invest?"*

Your brain is like an iceberg, and the logical part is the tiny tip that protrudes above the surface of the water. Yet your unconscious mind is much larger and more powerful, and that's the part below the water.

How can you engage the larger, more powerful unconscious part of your brain?

Ask a question and then let the unconscious part find the answer. If there is an investment question you're struggling with or pondering, just ask a question and await the answer.

In the time when you're not busy with work or thinking too intensely about a thousand other things, your subconscious brain will give you the answer.

Using your intuition to invest

There is an aspect of investing that goes beyond math and financial statements. With time, if you are to gain an advantage over other investors you must think in a way that diverges from the crowd, otherwise you could just get the market's return with an index.

Li Lu put it well: "Part of the game of investing is to come into your own. You must find some way that perfectly fits your personality because there is some element of a zero sum game in investing."[3]

He's saying that if you buy, someone else has to sell. And when you sell, somebody has to buy. One of you will be on the winning side of that trade, and you can't both be right. To win more than you lose you must develop an edge. Aim to be better informed than the person on the other side of the trade.

Great investors use their intuition

If investing only required insanely good math skills then all mathematicians could easily become billionaires. In fact, programmers who were good at artificial intelligence could craft algorithms to beat the market.

With incentives so high to best the market, and so many others working hard and smart to make money every day, an investor must think differently or possess intuition that others don't have.

I deeply believe that to beat the market, one needs intuition. It's not enough to be a quantitative thinker. Analysts are good at math and computers are even better.

Financial analysts don't know everything

A financial analyst uses math and data to predict cash flows and financial strength. But using these "left-brain" rational tools doesn't make you a good investor. If it did, anyone with a mathematical mind could become rich.

A deep understanding of companies requires an investor to look beyond facts and figures and embrace future possibilities. Fewer people have this kind of vision. In contrast, I have read many analyst reports written by people so mired in numbers that they missed the big picture.

Professional investors with years of experience make serious misjudgments because they rely heavily on numbers or projecting what they saw in the past into the future. That's a recipe for failure because everything changes.

I'm going to give you an example of this kind of mistake of projecting the past into the future. It centers around the mutual fund company Dodge & Cox Funds. They run about five mutual funds, and their investment policy committee has a long tradition of making thoughtful investment decisions. Also, their management fees are pretty low for an actively managed fund company.

To explain a serious mistake at Dodge & Cox, one need look no further than a decision that their investment committee made during the financial crisis in 2008. They made a series of bad investments in banks because the committee was under the erroneous belief that the government would protect financial institutions, as they had done in previous economic crises. Dodge & Cox' analysts did not understand that the government's protection of banks in the past would not happen the same way in the new crisis; this is a prime of example of the fact that you can't step in the same river twice.

Some investors avoided financial stocks

Nobody could have predicted what would happen during or after the financial crisis of 2008. However, there will be intuitive investors who had a feeling that there was a lot they didn't know. Let me reiterate the usefulness of this concept "you don't know as much as you think you do."

Let me share with you the words of an intelligent investor who expressed his uncertainly about financials many months before the financial crisis occurred. In January 2008, many months before the crisis, Ben Inker of GMO, a large Boston money-management firm, wrote an essay titled "Our Financial House of Cards." Inker wrote:

Wise investors should completely avoid financial stocks. "The magnitude of the unknowns is such that we mere mortal analysts cannot hope to know what the true values of the companies are."

Managers at Dodge & Cox should have read Inker's essay,

because GMO is a well-known firm and their letters are read by many expert money managers. It's a serious mistake for any investment professional to either be unaware of the risks Inker described or to ignore them.

During the financial crisis, Dodge & Cox Stock Fund bought stocks of several financial companies because their prices had declined significantly, yet the fund managers thought the prices had declined more than their fundamentals had deteriorated. It was an ugly situation and Dodge & Cox investors (I was one of them) collectively lost billions of dollars because of the heavy bets on stocks they thought they understood, but didn't. Another way of putting it is that they lacked the intuition to grasp how little they knew about the assets they were buying.

As financial stock prices plunged in the second half of 2007 and the first half of 2008, Dodge & Cox was buying. By June 2008, Dodge & Cox Stock Fund was overweight in financials, with a 17% allocation, compared to 14% in the index. In the letter to shareholders reporting on the second quarter of 2008, the managers wrote: "We have selectively expanded the Fund's financials weighting because in our opinion their valuations have declined more than their underlying long-term fundamentals have deteriorated."[4]

That was a serious mistake, as the warning had appeared clear as day in Inker's essay many months before the financial crisis occurred: *"Wise investors should completely avoid financial stocks."* Dodge and Cox may have missed that essay, because for some reason they increased their holdings in financials.

Following the collapse of Lehman Brothers in September, the government's central bank intervened and virtually wiped out the bank's shareholders, like Dodge & Cox.[5] Dodge & Cox's chairman, John Gunn said, "The government, by its actions, destroyed capital in the financial institutions and discouraged private capital. It threw gasoline on the fire."

I understand Gunn's perspective that the government destroyed capital in the financial institutions, but I think that's like blaming firefighters for damaging the furniture when they put out an inferno. One attitude when something is big and dangerous is to stay a long way away from it. Other people want to come as close as possible without going in; that's a very tricky thing to do. I think Dodge & Cox played with financial fire without understanding the danger.

While Gunn accurately describes the government's actions as destroying capital, I think his complaint misses the gravity of the situation. Munger stated that the massive interference from the central bank during the financial crisis was necessary. "I admire the politicians who did it, and the technocrats including the Federal Reserve people, and I think it was absolutely required in that the dangers they were avoiding were worse than the troubles they caused."[6]

FORTY-SIX

DODGE & COX ANALYSTS DIDN'T SEE WHAT OTHERS SAW

MY POINT in describing this situation is to show that Dodge & Cox did not see problems that were evident to other intuitive investors. I like the fund company and I've been an investor in their funds for more than 20 years. But I do want to point out that if their analysts and managers had used intuition, they could have steered clear of the hazards in the road ahead before crashing into them head-on. If you trust your own intuition maybe you can avoid mistakes too.

Dodge & Cox failed to grasp the possibility of a systemic collapse and were thus unable to identify the worst-case scenarios.

But some people recognized the statistical outliers—possible but improbable events that can be hugely disruptive and destructive if they occur. Nassim Nicholas Taleb's "The Black Swan"[1] was published before the financial crisis and predicted the types of destructive events that followed.

For years, Grantham, Mayo, & van Otterloo's Jeremy Grantham observed the "slow-motion train wreck" in financials, and he explains why he felt a small group of investors anticipated the 100-year storm. "They're all right-brained: more intuitive, more given to developing odd theories," he wrote. "They are almost universally interested—

even obsessed—with outlier events, and unique, new and different combinations of factors."[2]

Intuitive types needed

In a 2009 article published after the financial crisis, Kiplinger's Finance Magazine noted that "Dodge & Cox could benefit from adding some intuitive, right-brained types to a staff replete with left-brained Stanford and Harvard graduates. That might help the firm anticipate the next 100-year storm before it hits."[3]

FORTY-SEVEN
NO CRYSTAL BALL

I HAVE no crystal ball and there's no way I can predict the next recession. But I have learned to listen to my intuition. Sometimes you can get overwhelmed looking at too many stocks and miss the gem right in front of you.

For example, I admired Amazon for a long time. I was a customer for more than 10 years before I ever bought stock in the company. I could see the amazing selection, the fast delivery, and the unparalleled customer service the company provided, yet I still invested in other companies.

From 2000 to 2005, it was not obvious to everyone how successful Amazon and Google would become. Many questioned whether these companies would even become profitable. I didn't invest in Amazon or Google even though I was using them all the time. My early blind spot as an investor was being distrustful of my intuition.

FORTY-EIGHT

YOU CAN DO THIS!

YOU CAN BECOME A FAR BETTER investor by exercising your intuition. Think about it like getting a workout. At first you might be out of breath or your body will feel sore. But the more you trust your intuition, the better you'll get at using it.

Be patient with yourself and don't worry about experimenting with stocks where your intuition feels something - even if you can't rationally explain it. Just start small when you're experimenting.

No matter what happens, you will learn: if the stock goes up, you profit, and if your experiment fails, you pick failure's pocket and learn a lesson.

If you take anything with you at all from this section, I hope you'll remember the following:

- Trust your intuition to get beyond thinking.
- Your intuition will help you steer clear of problems and find opportunities. You know more than you think.

- As a loyal customer of a company, your intuition may provide a unique perspective.

CONCLUSION

In the introduction I wrote that I went from being a bad investor to a good investor when I started investing with index funds.

To be specific, I did best and kept things simple with mostly investments. I started with $100 each month, but that was so easy that I graduated to $200. When you do a set amount at intervals it's so simple: the perfect minimalist approach. It makes sure you participate and takes the human tendency to time the market out of the equation.

I traveled down Brazil in the fall of 1999 and stayed until the following spring. While I was there I photographed Randas Batista, the renowned Brazilian heart surgeon, and I wrote about my adventures in an online journal, Jeffrey Luke's Brazil Diary.[1]

Dr. Randas Batista, the renown heart surgeon in Curitiba, Brazil. I was in Brazil to photograph Dr. Batista in the operating room and when I wasn't photographing surgery I traveled the country taking pictures and writing about the people I met. Photo by Jeff Luke.

When I left for my travels I bought a few blank checks and envelopes so I could keep investing while I was on the road — these were the days before all mutual fund companies had easy ways to invest online.

This monthly investing habit has become much easier with

brokerage apps that make investing with your phone a cinch. Phones didn't have apps or Internet back in 1999 and 2000, yet I still managed to find a post office or mailbox to keep to stay on schedule.

My returns over the years have been good because of this habit. It didn't matter if the market was up or down, I just kept investing. I have a learned a lot about investing since then, but I wouldn't say my results have improved. The mistakes I made were mainly when I departed from the mostly investments and I would have been better off if I'd just stuck to it. I know why I left index fund investing: I was attracted by the challenge of picking stocks, which is something I still enjoy. However, I know my whole program lost several years of progress during the time I thought I was being smart and left index investing by the wayside.

I hope this book helps you learn to invest. You can get a perfectly decent long-term result by investing at regular intervals. Your future self will thank you.

THANK YOU!

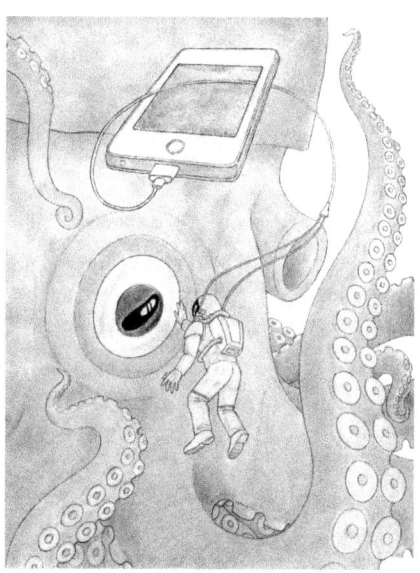

Art by Edwin Yaguar Chávez

If you enjoyed this book and feel it would be helpful to other readers, *can I ask you for a quick favor?*

If you can find a minute today to leave a short review on the *Winvesting* page at Amazon, I would be very grateful.

This is a new book, and I hope you found it useful and learned something along the way.

As a new author, your review will help others get a feel for whether the book will be useful to them before they spend money on the purchase.

I appreciate you taking the time to leave a review, and I know future readers will too.

Thanks so much!

Jeff Luke

ABOUT THE AUTHOR

Jeff Luke lives and works as a photographer and writer in Seattle, Washington. His photography has appeared in *The New York Times* and other publications worldwide.

Winvesting is one of several books about investing. Other titles include *Why I Should Start Trading in ETFs* (2020), *Stock Market Success* (2016), *Stock Market Intelligence* (2018), *Smart Stocks* (2019), and *Winvesting* (2020).

His book "Animal Donut: Images & Stories" features artistic photos of animals & donuts, which you can see at his website: animaldonut.com and on Instagram @animaldonut

He enjoys biking, photography, writing, and taking his husky buddies Maximus and Snowy for walks along the lake.

If you have any questions or would just like to connect, please email jlukephoto@gmail.com

---

Disclosure: At the time of publishing the author owns the following index funds and stocks mentioned in this book[1]:

- Vanguard Emerging Markets Index Fund (VEMAX)
- Vanguard S&P 500 Index (VFIAX)
- Amazon.com
- Berkshire Hathaway

- Carmax
- Waters

ALSO BY JEFF LUKE

Stock Market Intelligence (2018)

This was my first major book about picking stocks. It introduced the PALMS investing system to help people just starting out figure out the five questions to ask before buying any stock.

Smart Stocks (2019)

This book expands on the PALMS investing system introduced in my first book, and it dives into how to read annual reports and invest in stocks of small companies.

The ETF Investor (2020)

This book shows why exchange-traded funds (ETFs) are a simple way for investors with any level of experience can get started with this easy way to instantly own a diverse portfolio of stocks.

Beginning with a few simple ETF approaches to help investors just starting out, the book dives deep into exploring 19 ETFs they might not have yet discovered.

CONNECT

If there's anything you wish you could learn about investing but didn't find in these pages, just send me an email and I'll consider including the material in a future edition.

    email: jlukephoto@gmail.com

    Thanks for taking the time to read this book. I appreciate your time and look forward to hearing from you.

NOTES

2. Basic Facts About Index Funds

1. The S&P 500 index fund tracks the Standard & Poor's 500 index. This is a benchmark against which all investment performance can be compared. It's a way for investment managers to see if they are doing better or worse than the average of the 500 largest companies in the United States.
2. Vanguard is a mutual fund company that offers a variety of different mutual funds. The Vanguard S&P 500 index fund is one of their most popular funds. These are the fund's 10 largest holdings as of 12/31/2019.
3. Even though the fund is called the S&P 500 Index Fund, there are actually 509 stocks in this fund because some stocks have different share classes, such as "A" shares and "B" shares. You don't have to know all the details about these, but this explains why the fund has slightly more than 500 stocks in it.
4. Fund holdings as of 12/31/2019 as published on the Vanguard website: https://investor.vanguard.com/mutual-funds/profile/portfolio/vfiax
5. Fund holdings as of 12/31/2019 as published on Sequoia Fund's website. https://www.sequoiafund.com/Performance
6. An annual expense ratio is the ongoing expense that investors pay the fund company to manage their money. It pays for fund expenses and management fees. This fee is automatically removed from your investment. Fund expenses are one of the only aspects of investing you can control.
7. Vanguard Fund holdings as of 12/31/2019: https://investor.vanguard.com/mutual-funds/profile/portfolio/vfiax and Sequoia Fund holdings as of 12/31/2019: https://www.sequoiafund.com/Performance
8. Active fund managers trail the S&P 500 for the ninth year in a row in triumph of indexing - CNBC - March 15, 2019 https://www.cnbc.com/2019/03/15/active-fund-managers-trail-the-sp-500-for-the-ninth-year-in-a-row-in-triumph-for-indexing.html

3. Where Can You Buy Index Funds & ETFs?

1. Vanguard website: ETFs vs. mutual funds: A comparison https://investor.vanguard.com/etf/etf-vs-mutual-fund
2. Vanguard's investor website: https://investor.vanguard.com/etf/faqs
3. Vanguard's investor website: https://investor.vanguard.com/etf/faqs
4. ETFs vs. mutual funds: A comparison. https://investor.vanguard.com/etf/etf-vs-mutual-fund
5. Can you reinvest your capital gains distributions? - Vanguard Investor News -

December 21, 2018 https://investornews.vanguard/why-do-etfs-pay-capital-gains/

4. How to Invest in Index Funds

1. You can choose other fund companies or brokerage firms, but Vanguard has a unique structure. "At Vanguard, there are no outside owners, and therefore, no conflicting loyalties. The company is owned by its funds, which in turn are owned by their shareholders—including you, if you're a Vanguard fund investor." -From vanguard.com

8. Ted & Todd's Returns Almost Beat the S&P 500 Index

1. 1CNBC's Becky Quick interviews Warren Buffett (2/25/19)

9. You Get What You Don't Pay For

1. I heard this saying from Jack Bogle, the founder of The Vanguard Funds.

10. The Mighty Sequoia

1. The 6 Greatest Mutual Fund Managers Of The Last Decade To Use Now by Ken Kam, Forbes June 1, 2018 https://www.forbes.com/sites/kenkam/2018/06/01/the-6-greatest-mutual-fund-managers-of-the-last-decade-to-use-now/#78376002e678

11. I Wanted to Invest in Sequoia

1. Sequoia Fund Tries to Recover from Valiant Misstep https://www.kiplinger.com/article/investing/T041-C009-S002-sequoia-fund-tries-to-recover.html
2. Sequoia Fund Tries to Recover from Valiant Misstep https://www.kiplinger.com/article/investing/T041-C009-S002-sequoia-fund-tries-to-recover.html

12. Sequoia Fund Disaster

1. Valeant: A timeline of the Big Pharma scandal. Fortune Magazine, October 31, 2015 by Stephen Gandel
2. Drug company Valeant (VRX) was one of Wall Street's hottest stocks for years. It was seemingly all based on a new business model. CEO Michael Pearson believed

that drug companies were terribly inefficient in spending money on research and development that often went nowhere.

Pearson had a new plan: Create a drug giant that focused on distribution, and let someone else do the research. The plan was controversial and required rapid acquisitions to make it work. So Pearson started buying up rival drug companies, firing staff, and slashing R&D. That was unpopular in the drug industry. And it also led the company to pile on debt. But it seemed to work for a while. Valeant's stock rose and rose to a high of $260.

But in the past month, allegations have surfaced that Valeant's true success may have been built on something else: Price gouging, a secret network of specialty pharmacies, and fraud. "Valeant: A Timeline of the Big Pharma Scandal" https://fortune.com/2015/10/31/valeant-scandal/

3. https://www.kiplinger.com/article/investing/T041-C009-S002-sequoia-fund-tries-to-recover.html
4. "Valeant: A Timeline of the Big Pharma Scandal" https://fortune.com/2015/10/31/valeant-scandal/
5. Sequoia Fund 3rd Quarter 2019 Quarterly Fact Sheet as of 9/30/2019

13. The Lesson You Can Learn

1. From Morningstar.com https://www.morningstar.com/funds/xnas/sequx/quote

14. Once Great Actively Managed Funds That Flopped

1. Global Value Investor David Winters Raises the Alarm About the Flood of Money Pouring into Index Funds [https://wealthtrack.com/global-value-investor-david-winters-raises-alarm-flood-money-pouring-index-funds/#more-16806] [https://www.investmentnews.com/section/video?playerType=CMWealth&bctid=5496805417001&date=20170707]
2. Wintergreen Fund Supplement to Prospectus and Summary Prospectus each dated April 30, 2018, as amended https://www.sec.gov/Archives/edgar/data/1326544/000089418919002203/wintergreen_497e.htm
3. Famed Value Investor David Winters Is Shutting Down His Wintergreen Fund https://www.barrons.com/articles/david-winters-shuts-down-wintergreen-fund-51556053428
4. https://www.cnbc.com/2015/03/02/cnbc-excerpts-billionaire-investor-warren-buffett-on-cnbcs-squawk-box-today.html
5. Muhlenkamp expense ratio as of 12/10/2019 on Morningstar https://www.morningstar.com/funds/xnas/muhlx/quote
6. https://www.morningstar.com/funds/xnas/fairx/quote
7. "Legg Mason's Bill Miller leaves firm amid faded glory" https://www.reuters.com/article/us-legg-mason-miller/legg-masons-bill-miller-leaves-firm-amid-faded-glory-idUSKCN10M1DV
8. https://www.morningstar.com/funds/xnas/cgmfx/quote

18. Focus with Funds

1. Each of these index funds has a corresponding ETF. The actual holdings of the ETF mirror the index fund, so you're getting the same stocks. Only the container is different. For example, VFIAX = VOO. VTIAX = VXUS. VEMAX = VWO. While the stock holdings are identical, the ETF has a slightly lower annual expense in some cases.

20. Portfolio #2

1. https://youtu.be/MjwJNoeGuNE
2. The Only Person Besides Warren Buffett Who Charlie Munger Trusts With His Money - QZ.com - https://qz.com/work/1551328/the-only-person-besides-warren-buffett-who-charlie-munger-trusts-with-his-money/
3. Vanguard's website portfolio page for Vanguard Emerging Markets Stock Index Fund (VEMAX) as of 11/30/2019.
4. Disclosure: The author owns shares of Vanguard Emerging Markets Stock Index Fund (VEMAX).

21. Portfolio #3

1. I use the word "funds" here, but it's synonymous with ETFs. Investors can either buy sector funds or ETFs, as the stock holdings in a fund company's sector index funds and ETFs should have identical holdings. You may want to check first to verify that these holdings are identical, but for the purposes of this book, the word "fund" is used and can be substituted with "ETF".

22. Chocolate, Vanilla, or Swirl?

1. Vanguard Total World Stock Fund Admiral Shares (WTWAX) as of 11/30/2019.
2. Percentages of Vanguard Total World Stock Fund Admiral Shares (WTWAX) as of 11/30/2019.
3. Percentages of Vanguard Total World Stock Fund Investor Shares (WTWAX) as of 11/30/2019.
4. As of 11/30/2019

23. Sector Funds

1. Vanguard's website portfolio page for Vanguard Emerging Markets Stock Index Fund (VEMAX) as of 11/30/2019.
2. Vanguard website as of 12/31/2019

NOTES   171

3. Vanguard website: https://investor.vanguard.com/etf/profile/portfolio/VEA/quarter-end-holdings
4. Vanguard's website description for Vanguard Health Care ETF (VHT) as of 11/30/2019
5. XBI ETF overview https://www.etf.com/XBI#overview
6. For this fund I'm noting the ETF instead of the index fund, because the index fund has a minimum initial investment of $100,000, but you can buy the VGT ETF for the price of one share, which was $187.15 as of 3/20/2020.
7. Holdings as of 12/31/2019
8. For this fund I'm noting the ETF instead of the index fund, because the index fund has a minimum initial investment of $100,000, but you can buy the VCR ETF for the price of one share, which was $128.83 as of 3/20/2020.
9. Holdings as of 12/31/2019

28. Investing vs. Gambling

1. Robinhood is a mobile app that lets people trade for free. "Hacking" is figuring out some sketchy way to do something that is probably against the rules. "Paper" is slang for money. "Chicken tendies" are chicken tenders, a popular end goal of many participants on Wall Street Bets, an online message board on Reddit.com. You're better off not going there.
2. "One Up on Wall Street," by Peter Lynch and John Rothchild, Simon & Schuster, 1989

33. Come Into Your Own

1. Li Lu is a brilliant investor who has his own investing company called Himalaya Capital and is referred to as the "Warren Buffett of China." He has earned the admiration of many, including Charlie Munger, who admires the rationality and discipline he applies to his work. https://www.brainyquote.com/authors/li-lu-quotes
2. Buffett's exception to this rule was his foray into investing in tech with Berkshire Hathaway's purchase of IBM stock in 2011.

34. Coming into My Own: Amazon

1. Charlie Munger's advice on investing and life choices https://youtu.be/RFxXl9eAWV4

38. Find Fat Pitches

1. Li Lu quote from Poor Charlie's Almanack, 3rd edition 2009, page 61 on Himalaya Capital "Investment Philosophy" section of website: http://www.himalayacapital.com/investphil.htm

39. Become More Productive

1. "How to be More Productive" - video by Essential Craftsman on YouTube https://youtu.be/qP1AmDRhoas
2. "Influence: The Psychology of Persuasion," by Robert Cialdini, Harper Business 2006 https://www.amazon.com/Influence-Psychology-Persuasion-Robert-Cialdini/dp/006124189X
3. 10 Ways You Can Think and Succeed Like Charlie Munger - https://www.vintagevalueinvesting.com/10-ways-you-can-think-and-succeed-like-charlie-munger/

40. Investing Tools: Stock Punch Card

1. One of the investing greats explains his portfolio strategy: https://insight.kellogg.northwestern.edu/article/investment-great-lou-simpson-explains-portfolio-strategy
2. Why Warren Buffett's '20-Slot Rule' will make you insanely successful and wealthy - March 16, 2017 cnbc.com https://www.cnbc.com/2017/03/16/warren-buffetts-20-slot-rule-will-make-you-successful-and-wealthy.html

41. I Accidentally Smashed My iPhone

1. Data from SEC Website, investor.gov, where you can use their compound interest calculator to enter different investment amounts, annual returns, and time frames to find out how your money compounds over time. https://www.investor.gov/additional-resources/free-financial-planning-tools/compound-interest-calculator
2. When I first owned Leucadia, it was run by Ian Cumming and Joseph Steinberg, two investors with a solid long-term record. Soon after I invested they merged their company with an investment bank named Jefferies Group. The combined entity had a new CEO and has delivered poor performance for many years since.

43. Big Things Start Small

1. The crucial mindset of Jeff Bezos says that to innovate you have to experiment, and because some experiments take time one should think long-term by Ruth

Umoh, November 29, 2017 cnbc.com https://www.cnbc.com/2017/11/09/jeff-bezos-says-you-should-have-this-mindset-to-be-successful.html

44. Stepping in Rivers

1. "This is the last article you'll ever need to read on market timing." MarketWatch https://www.marketwatch.com/story/this-is-the-last-article-youll-ever-need-to-read-on-market-timing-analyst-claims-2019-02-06
2. Two days before going to press the stock market continued its bear market fall and the Dow lost 2,997 points on Monday, March 16, 2020. These are times an investor wants to be prepared for so they can invest when stocks go on sale.

45. Intuitive Investing

1. These insights into intuition are explained in Gavin de Becker's YouTube video, "The Gift of Fear" https://youtu.be/zNtXjIiJoPU
2. This example of why people are fascinated about car accidents is from Gavin de Becker's YouTube video, "The Gift of Fear" https://youtu.be/zNtXjIiJoPU
3. Li Lu on his investing process: https://acquirersmultiple.com/2017/11/li-lu-investing-is-about-intellectual-honesty-know-what-you-dont-know/
4. What Went Wrong at Dodge & Cox, Andrew Tanzer, Kiplinger Magazine, February 1, 2009https://www.kiplinger.com/article/investing/T033-C000-S002-what-went-wrong-at-dodge-cox.html
5. What Went Wrong at Dodge & Cox, Andrew Tanzer, Kiplinger Magazine, February 1, 2009https://www.kiplinger.com/article/investing/T033-C000-S002-what-went-wrong-at-dodge-cox.html
6. Berkshire Hathaway VP Charlie Munger on investing https://www.youtube.com/watch?v=peUrLZ24GfM&t=51s

46. Dodge & Cox Analysts Didn't See What Others Saw

1. The Black Swan: The Impact of the Highly Improbable by Nassim Nicholas Taleb, April 3, 2008 https://www.amazon.com/Black-Swan-Improbable-Robustness-Fragility/dp/081297381X
2. Jeremy Grantham Quarterly Letter, "Reaping the Whirlwind" October 2008 https://www.scribd.com/document/7514391/Jeremy-Grantham-Quarterly-Letter-Reaping-the-Whirlwind
3. What Went Wrong at Dodge & Cox? by Andrew Tanzer, Kiplinger's Magazine, February 1, 2009 https://www.kiplinger.com/article/investing/T033-C000-S002-what-went-wrong-at-dodge-cox.html

Conclusion

1. If you'd like to read about my adventures in Brazil you can Google "Jeffrey Luke's Brazil Diary" and click the first result. If you're reading this on a mobile device you can use this link: http://www.jeffreyluke.com/Brazil_Diary/Brazil_Diary_preface.html

About the Author

1. Holdings as of May 15, 2020.

www.ingramcontent.com/pod-product-compliance
Lightning Source LLC
Chambersburg PA
CBHW052354220526
45465CB00003BA/1099